MOONSHINE

A Celebration of America's Original Rebel Spirit

JOHN SCHLIMM

Cocktail Photographs by
AMY BEADLE ROTH

CITADEL PRESS
Kensington Publishing Corp.
www.kensingtonbooks.com

To the extent recipes in this book include ingredients identified by the trademarks owned by others, no endorsement of this book or the recipes by such owners is suggested or implied, and all rights of every kind in and to such trademarks remain with the respective trademark owners.

CITADEL PRESS BOOKS are published by

Kensington Publishing Corp.
119 West 40th Street
New York, NY 10018

Copyright © 2018 John Schlimm

Design and production by Koechel Peterson and Associates, Minneapolis, Minnesota

All rights reserved. No part of this book may be reproduced in any form or by any means without the prior written consent of the publisher, excepting brief quotes used in reviews.

All Kensington titles, imprints, and distributed lines are available at special quantity discounts for bulk purchases for sales promotions, premiums, fund-raising, educational, or institutional use.

Special book excerpts or customized printings can also be created to fit specific needs. For details, write or phone the office of the Kensington sales manager: Kensington Publishing Corp., 119 West 40th Street, New York, New York 10018, attn.: Sales Department; phone 1-800-221-2647.

CITADEL PRESS and the Citadel logo are Reg. U.S. Pat. & TM Off.

ISBN-13: 978-0-8065-3919-5
ISBN-10: 0-8065-3919-4

First Citadel hardcover printing: October 2018

10 9 8 7 6 5 4 3 2 1

Printed in the United States of America

Library of Congress CIP data is available.

First electronic edition: October 2018

ISBN-13: 978-0-8065-3921-8
ISBN-10: 0-8065-3921-6

To the rebel spirit in each of us.

CONTENTS

PART 1: The Story of Moonshine

9

Moonshine by any other name...

White lightning, hooch, mountain dew, wildcat, skullpop, stump water, mother's milk, corn liquor, 'shine, tangleleg, soda pop moon, brush whiskey, white likker, panther sweat, widow maker, rise'n shine, tiger's sweat, blockade whiskey, yack yack bourbon, bootleg, corn squeezins, rotgut, bathtub gin, tiger spit, white mule, goat whiskey, city gin, bark whiskey, catdaddy, stumphole, skullcracker, Dubois Dew, block & tackle, paleface, firewater, kickapoo, panther piss, bush whiskey, mule kick, scorpion juice, jackass brandy, happy Sally, hillbilly pop, bust head, splo, homebrew, Kentucky mule, pine top, stump puller, Monongahela Rye, radiator whiskey, panther's breath, cool water, Straitsville Special, wildcat, demon rum, ruckus juice, alley bourbon, fortyrod, old horsey.

The Story of Moonshine

Moonshiners Hall of Fame

Robert Glenn "Junior" Johnson, Jr.

Son of one of the South's biggest moonshiners, at age 14, Junior Johnson was already outrunning the authorities to deliver his dad's homemade moonshine throughout North Carolina, including Wilkes County where he was born. This earned him an arrest at his dad's still and a jail sentence of one year and one day in 1956. As a moonshine runner, one of his signature moves was the 180.

Thanks to this back-road baptism by fire, Junior later became one of NASCAR's first superstars, winning fifty races during the 1950s and 1960s and later becoming a team owner in the 1970s and 1980s. Junior's life was the inspiration for the 1973 film *The Last America Hero*, which starred Jeff Bridges and was based on the *Esquire* article "Great Balls of Fire" written by Tom Wolfe. His efforts on the track also earned him a spot in the first class of inductees into the NASCAR Hall of Fame and a presidential pardon from Ronald Reagan.

Today, Johnson has his own legal brand of white lightning produced by Piedmont Distillers, Inc. called Midnight Moon Moonshine, which is inspired by his family's original recipe.

CHAPTER 1

An American Story

Homegrown corn, mountain spring water, sugar, and yeast. These are the ingredients of a uniquely American story.

The recipe for moonshine—unaged, clear whiskey—distilled on U.S. soil has remained the same for more than two centuries and across the threshold of a new millennium. And the history of moonshine embodies the tale of immigrants braving the unknown to forge life and freedom in a savage new land. It is high proof of their grit and savvy as they chased the same primal desire for a good life, liberty, and pursuit of happiness still rooted deeply within our hearts.

Moonshine is our link to the beginning of America as we know it. It is an ancestral handshake—preserved in a Mason jar and extended across the annals of history to each of us today.

Long before European immigrants settled in the Thirteen Colonies, Native Americans produced the first liquor using native plants, such as berries and fruits.

As far back as the fall of 1620, colonist George Thorpe, who co-founded Berkeley Hundred (now Berkeley Plantation)—on the north bank of the James River in current-day Charles City, Virginia, and site of the first Thanksgiving in 1619—distilled a batch of beer, but in fact it wasn't beer at all. This new concoction launched a spirited alternative to the popular home-brewed English ales chugged throughout the colonies at this time.

Thorpe's secret ingredient: native-grown corn from Powhatan Indians.

The result: the first corn whiskey, and a great-granddaddy to the all-American moonshine that would soon emerge and be the heirloom pride of moonshiners passed down through the generations.

"Wee have found a waie to make soe good drink of Indian corne," Thorpe triumphantly reported of his creation in a letter to his friend and Berkeley Hundred historian John Smyth.

Throughout the next century onward, more than two hundred thousand Scots-Irish immigrants mostly from the province of Ulster in Ireland—who knew their way around a good time, a fiddle, and a copper pot still—settled in Pennsylvania and downward into the central and southern portions of the Appalachian region—Virginia, the Carolinas, Kentucky, West Virginia, Georgia, and Tennessee. They came to escape religious persecution and drought, and to protest such laws as the English Malt Tax of 1725 and the Gin Tax of 1736 that threatened their livelihoods and revelry back home. However, these taxes and government influences were only a stark foreshadowing of what lay ahead for these optimistic new residents in the Thirteen Colonies.

Along with an aversion to oppressive government authority, these early moonshine immigrants brought with them a rich distilling heritage dating back centuries in Europe, artisanal skills, and their ages-old whiskey recipe for *uisce beatha*, which when translated from Irish Gaelic means "water of life."

During the 1700s, moonshiners in the northern colonies often used rye to make their whiskey, while corn remained the main ingredient in Southern moonshine.

The American South—especially the topography of Appalachia, which encompasses the regions spread throughout and around the Blue Ridge and Smokey Mountains—reminded these Scots-Irish pioneers of home. They were drawn to the untouched wilds of this new frontier. The carved-out hollows, bluffs, peaks, flatlands, and pristine streams winding through the ancient mountains of hardwood forests. The laurel and huckleberry, the honeysuckle, dogwood, and columbines. The fertile land teeming with wildlife—bald eagles, falcons, woodpeckers, wild turkeys, and songbirds; white-tailed deer, black bear, coyotes, otters, and shrews; brook trout and smallmouth bass.

When England and Scotland were merged under the Acts of Unions, and the English Malt Tax of 1725 was levied, distillers were forced out of business or underground. Many continued to produce their whisky secretly at night, which earned them their name—moonshiners—and their fluid masterpiece its name: moonshine. These terms also derive from the moonrakers, who were English smugglers, not unlike the American moonshiners and bootleggers who would follow.

Weary and exhausted from the journey of a lifetime, here the immigrants found a paradise off the beaten path where they could settle down and begin life anew, on their own terms. They had found a home at last.

These were folks for whom the land itself became a part of their souls. And the moonshine they wrought by hand from nature's purest bounty there—the farm-to-still corn, the freshest water—was akin to the very blood coursing through their veins.

The waves of immigrants populating the Thirteen Colonies, including those from countries like Germany, France, and England, were experts in fermentation and distillation—turning grains into whiskey and fruits into brandy. Their Old World talents for transforming a still into an instrument for creating art didn't originate in a textbook. Rather, moonshine was born from tradition, generation-to-generation apprenticing, trial and error, and, most importantly, the moonshiner's own hands.

For folks with little or no formal schooling, distilling—especially in its allergic-to-the-law incarnation as moonshining—offered a logical trade skill that played to every moonshiner's dirt-road street smarts and gutsy approach to securing a better life for their families. Moonshiners were backwoods inventors and craftsmen, and entrepreneurs. These were common, everyday men and women, who, in combining a grassroots ingenuity and perfection that only human hands can render, altered the course of American history.

In fact, ingenuity was a moonshiner's middle name. Still is. For example, while early batches of colonial moonshine proved a bit weak because of primitive equipment and impurities, resourceful moonshiners soon solved the problem. They discovered that running

Whisky vs. Whiskey

Regardless of the spelling, the word is of Celtic origin. Whisky: spelling used when referring to whisky in and from places like Scotland, Canada, China, and Japan. Whiskey: spelling used when referring to whiskey in the United States and Ireland. The spelling for moonshine, however, is universal!

the white lightning through the still three times, instead of one or two, guaranteed a 90-proof or better result. This next-generation moonshine that resulted was signified by "XXX" on the jug, letting revelers know forever after that they were getting their money's worth of a good buzz!

The process and equipment for making moonshine is little changed from the beginning: copper or steel stills, a barrel for water, and copper tubing.

Early moonshiners were free-spirited—a hallmark of living handed down along with every family's special moonshine recipe to the next of kin in line—and they took their craft to heart. As the classic early twentieth-century ballad "The Moonshiner" declares: "Moonshine dear moonshine, oh how I love thee."

It was love first that flowed from every still. The 'shine itself was only further proof of the

pride and adventurous nature that drove these pioneering artisans to advance their craft.

Once settled in the colonies, moonshiners shared their boozy knowhow with neighbors, morphing experiences, tips, and methods. They developed friendships and alliances, and a ring of cohorts they could trust when authorities closed in.

Soon, unaged whiskey—authentic all-American-made moonshine that would become a national staple enduring through good times and bad—flowed freely throughout the colonies like the crystal-clear mountain creeks along which it was often distilled.

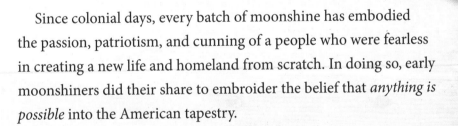

Moonshine was often used in folk medicine remedies. Combined with honey, lemon juice, and other fresh ingredients, it became a popular cold and cough syrup in colonial times.

Since colonial days, every batch of moonshine has embodied the passion, patriotism, and cunning of a people who were fearless in creating a new life and homeland from scratch. In doing so, early moonshiners did their share to embroider the belief that *anything is possible* into the American tapestry.

One batch of 'shine at a time, moonshiners as nation builders launched armies of free thinkers, leaders, and dreamers—and, yes, revolutionaries. At every step along the march of history, their efforts were paired with the original American outlaw they had perfected and that has fueled the can-do attitude of U.S. patriotism ever since.

Moonshiners Hall of Fame

Marvin "Popcorn" Sutton

With a signature hat and bib overalls, Popcorn Sutton was one of the twentieth century's most famous moonshiners, hailing from Cocke County, Tennessee, in the Great Smoky Mountains. With Scots-Irish blood flowing through his veins, he was an active moonshiner from the 1960s through the 2000s, a period that included multiple run-ins with the authorities while he quenched everyone's thirst with his homemade "likker."

Determined to bring his homespun wit and Tennessee white whiskey into the new millennium, Popcorn promoted his craft and batches of 'shine with a self-published memoir/how-to guide titled *Me and My Likker* and appearances in several documentaries—Neal Hutcheson's *This Is the Last Dam Run of Likker I'll Ever Make* (2002), *Mountain Talk* (2004), *The Last One* (2008), and *Popcorn Sutton: A Hell of a Life* (released in 2014 after Popcorn's death); and The History Channel's *Hillbilly: The Real Story* (2008). Documentary footage of Popcorn from Hutcheson was also used on Discovery Channel's *Moonshiners*, introducing the old-timer to a whole new audience and further establishing his reign as a moonshine king among kings.

Today, Popcorn's fans can legally enjoy a swig of his recipe thanks to Popcorn Sutton Distillery in Newport, TN, which produces The Original XXX Popcorn Sutton Small Batch Recipe.

CHAPTER 2

The Dawn of Moonshiners as Revolutionaries

From the early 1600s, the Thirteen Colonies were subjected to rules and laws limiting alcohol consumption. These ranged from controlling liquor sales in taverns to preventative measures for reining in the perceived evils of imbibing and public drunkenness. The restrictions were a slow ramping-up toward revolution; each constraint was like sticking a pin in the colonial consciousness, needling away public tolerance toward authority sip by sip.

By the 1770s, colonists each consumed more than six gallons of alcohol annually.

Among the more notable regulations:

In 1629, the Virginia Colonial Assembly declared: "Ministers shall not give themselves to excess in drinkinge, or riott, or spending their tyme idellye day or night."

In 1633, Plymouth Colony forbade "more than 2 pence worth" of spirits being sold to anyone other than "strangers just arrived."

In 1637, Massachusetts ordered that folks could not stay in a tavern "longer than necessary occasions."

In 1672, a law prevented alcohol from being used to pay wages. As a result, one of the first labor strikes ensued.

In 1679, Massachusetts formed the office of tithingman to monitor alcohol consumption and spotlight any liquor violations in colonists' homes.

Laws even prohibited the sale of liquor to Native Americans. Plus, fines and penalties were levied against those who were discovered drunk in public, and included other behavior such as gossiping— often two birds of a feather.

Minister John Wesley especially decried the wickedness of distilling throughout first his native England and later the Thirteen Colonies. He chastised both drinkers and liquor sellers. In a December 9, 1772 letter to the editor of *Lloyd's Evening Post* titled "Thoughts on the Present Scarcity of Provisions," he declared liquor a "deadly poison—poison that naturally destroys, not only the strength and life, but also the morals of our countrymen."

Wesley's solution to this evildoing was "prohibiting for ever that bane of health, that destroyer of strength, of life, and of virtue, distilling." This theme snaked its way throughout his sermons and those of his staunchest contemporaries. Pontifications like this on the immorality of alcohol and drunkenness relegated colonists to the razor-sharp precipice between heaven and hell.

The message: Change your drunken ways or be damned.

This was also the era of fire-and-brimstone preachers like Jonathan Edwards, who delivered his famous "Sinners in the Hands of an Angry God" sermon. Also, George Whitefield, whose advocacy for the Great Awakening throughout the colonies rocked folks— and their favorite boozy thirst quenchers—to the core. Among Whitefield's most famous revivalist preaching was "The Heinous Sin of Drunkenness" in which he methodically enumerated the case against imbibing: "SIXTH reason against the sin of drunkenness; it absolutely unfits a man for the enjoyment of God in heaven, and exposes him to his eternal wrath."

This was the puritanical origin of the temperance efforts that would one day target moonshiners and cement their reputation as ultimate rebels.

However, the tipping point came later in the eighteenth century, when the combustible combination of war and angry, disenfranchised citizens led to outright revolt.

On the heels of the French and Indian War (1754 to 1763), Great Britain decided the Thirteen Colonies should kick in their fair share of the resulting war debt. The British forces had protected the colonies from the French military, and now the Crown wanted an even greater commitment of loyalty and money in return. With previous experience in the area of taxing liquor and other goods, Great Britain cast a lustful eye toward whiskey production in the colonies. The English deemed this the surest, quickest way to squeeze more money from strapped colonists under their control.

Moonshiners also referred to themselves as blockaders, who believed it was their God-given right to produce their white lightning free of government control.

Squashed beneath this prickly thumb, the colonists declared enough is enough. Taxing liquor to line the Crown's pockets provoked bad memories and proved the final straw amid mounting tension between an out-of-touch British ruling class and everyday merchants and farmers. The immigrants did not brave more than three thousand miles of an unrelenting Atlantic Ocean in search of a new life in an untamed foreign land only to be wrenched backward into submission. Contributing their fair share was one thing, but being treated unfairly was unacceptable.

Angry colonial merchants, moonshiners, and their customers realized that the mantle of change was now squarely on their shoulders. The first protests and boycotts against British government and products began. Colonists now understood that the independence they desired, especially pertaining to the sale and jovial swigs of XXX, would depend upon their willingness to take a stand and fight for their voices to be heard, even at an ultimate cost.

From the moment the Sons of Liberty—a secret society organized to protect the rights of colonists and oppose British laws and taxes— transformed Boston Harbor into the world's largest teapot on December 16, 1773, they proved to be a new breed of pioneer. This was a unified citizenry unlike the world had ever seen. Their badge of honor was marked by a fierce and visionary drive toward one goal: freedom.

Their motto: No taxation without representation.

Their clear message: Don't mess with us!

Samuel Adams, a chief architect of the Boston Tea Party and a Sons of Liberty leader, declared: "Among the natural rights of the Colonists are these: First, a right to life; Secondly, to liberty; Thirdly, to property; together with the right to support and defend them in the best manner they can. . . . and in case of intolerable oppression, civil or religious, to leave the society they belong to, and enter into another."

Moonshiners especially had found their battle cry in these tenets. They were ready to become citizen-soldiers in the coming battle.

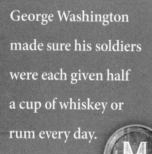

George Washington made sure his soldiers were each given half a cup of whiskey or rum every day.

Spurred onward by the events and emerging new leaders of the day, colonists soon created their own Continental Congress, which met in three variations from 1774 to 1789. They established a Continental Army on July 14, 1775, as well as state militias, under the leadership of General George Washington. As a result of this groundwork, the colonists successfully mounted the most famous revolution in the history of the world.

Independence, including the future of moonshining, was now up for grabs. It all came down to which side could outwit, outlast, and outfight in order to claim victory. *Big risk, big return* was a concept reared by these patriots and sewn into the very fabric of the moonshiner's credo from this moment forward.

From 1765 to 1783, the American Revolution was waged across storied battlefields such as Lexington and Concord, Saratoga, and

Yorktown. Moonshiners left their families back in the hills, hollows, and small towns, just as other patriots did, taking up arms to secure their right to produce magic in a still.

A pinnacle moment came midway through the war with the masterful crafting of the Declaration of Independence by the Committee of Five—lead author Thomas Jefferson, along with John Adams, Ben Franklin, Robert R. Livingston, and Roger Sherman. The statement was formally adopted by the Second Continental Congress on July 4, 1776.

What emerged from Jefferson's declaratory pen was pure poetry that would be evermore committed to memory by proud and free Americans, including moonshiners who would themselves exert their own declarations of independence

John Adams

Founding Father, and future president, John Adams enjoyed swigs of hard cider every day.

many times in the coming years: "We hold these truths to be self-evident, that all men are created equal, that they are endowed by their Creator with certain unalienable rights, that among these are life, liberty and the pursuit of happiness. That to secure these rights, governments are instituted among men, deriving their just powers from the consent of the governed. That whenever any form of government becomes destructive to these ends, it is the right of the people to alter or to abolish it, and to institute new government, laying its foundation on such principles and organizing its powers in such form, as to them shall seem most likely to effect their safety and happiness."

Three of the fifty-six signers of the Declaration of Independence—Matthew Thornton, James Smith, and George Taylor—were originally from Ulster, which was the area from which many of the first moonshiners had immigrated.

Embracing these principles, the colonists fought even harder, sacrificed even more, and eventually prevailed in securing their independence from Great Britain in 1783. But victory and freedom came at a staggering cost to the United States: nearly seven thousand soldiers were killed in battle and millions of dollars in expenses marked not only the price tag strung around the neck of a new nation, but also the birth of its national debt.

Also around this time, Founding Father and a signer of the Declaration of Independence Benjamin Rush delivered a slap across the face of every moonshiner and their customers when he published a 1784 tract titled *An Inquiry into the Effects of Ardent Spirits upon the Human Body and Mind*. Americans had transitioned from drinking weaker brews and other alcohol in colonial days to the current and much stronger XXX-proof moonshine, and Rush proclaimed this shift physically and mentally detrimental to citizens. He labeled drunkenness an "odious disease."

Rush's claims took root in conservative and religious minds, launching a more formal temperance movement throughout the country. Moonshiners were now seen even more clearly by these early temperance activists as distillers of doom and ill health. In the coming years and decades, this effort would be formalized into state associations and societies—a path that would eventually lead to Prohibition almost a century and a half later.

On March 4, 1789, the United States Constitution became the new supreme law of the land. Upon this triumphant milestone, Ben Franklin articulated a new rallying cry for colonists who were now basking on the doorstep of a promising future: "The Constitution only gives people the right to pursue happiness. You have to catch it yourself."

No one took these words-to-live-by to heart more seriously than the moonshiners. The future was theirs to catch and embrace, and happiness was theirs to distill and release to the masses.

But there was an unexpected hitch in this bright shiny horizon for moonshiners. A roadblock they never saw coming until it was too late.

As a result of the war debt and its related recession, in 1791, the U.S. Congress, under President George Washington and Treasury

George Washington remained nonpartisan throughout his presidency, but Alexander Hamilton veered deep into a fiscally sound and nationalistic philosophy that launched the country's first political party, the Federalist Party.

Secretary Alexander Hamilton, levied a federal tax called the Act of 1791 on liquor and spirits. Hamilton, especially, was not a fan of moonshiners and other distillers, and would soon zero in on them like a hunter stalking prey.

Nicknamed the Whiskey Tax and justified by Hamilton as a luxury tax—and by others as a sin tax—this was the first U.S. tax to be placed on a domestic product. It would also be the first major internal struggle of a nation, testing the U.S. Constitution in the face of crisis while pitting neighbor against neighbor.

For moonshiners, the Whiskey Tax was a sucker punch to the gut, especially for those who had fought in the War for Independence. They had returned home veterans and were among the first of the great American heroes in uniform. Now these back-hill distillers were about to be turned into something far different in the eyes of their government. They were about to become outlaws, criminals, and degenerates of society on a whole new level.

A shadow was cast and was encroaching on the stills that dotted the woodland landscapes throughout the South and beyond. The fight-or-flight time of reckoning had come.

George Washington

George Washington was a distiller himself. Thanks to the urging of his Scottish-born farm manager, James Anderson, Washington's Mount Vernon estate boasted what would become the country's largest commercial distillery. Washington's distillery opened in 1797, and hit its peak in 1799—the year of Washington's death—with five copper pot stills and an output of eleven thousand gallons of legal whiskey.

Moonshiners Hall of Fame

Maggie Bailey

In the dry community of Clovertown in Harlan County, Kentucky, moonshiner Maggie Bailey sold batches of white lightning from the time she was seventeen until she was ninety-five. She initially got in the business to help support her family that included five younger siblings. Known to many as the "Queen of the Mountain Bootleggers," Maggie was a very respected and generous neighbor—especially to those down on their luck. And she was no stranger to the law, having once been convicted and spent a year and a half in prison. Otherwise, Maggie beat the law dozens of time because of her grandmotherly charm and the fact everyone took an immediate liking to her.

CHAPTER 3

The Whiskey Rebellion

The Whiskey Tax of 1791 required distillers to pay either an annual lump sum of sixty cents per gallon per still capacity—an option which favored the bigger distillers—or nine cents per gallon of the whiskey actually produced—which was usually the way small distillers and farmer-moonshiners had to pay.

This resulted in the small distillers forking over almost three cents more per gallon in taxes. Also, the tax had to be paid in cash. For farmer-moonshiners who were barely making ends meet as it was, this was a fatal blow. Many of these folks supplemented their meager farming income—especially during lean years—by moonlighting as moonshiners.

For many impoverished farmer-moonshiners, transforming their crops, especially excess crops, into whiskey wasn't about luxury, but instead was a mode of survival. One bushel of corn could be distilled into two to three gallons of whiskey. Whiskey fetched a bigger profit than the corn alone. Also, whiskey was easier to transport over crude roads through thick forests, plus it could even be used as currency in exchange for needed supplies—food, tools, ammunition. Additionally, the mush of grain or fruit—called pot-tail—leftover in the stills could be recycled as feed for their livestock.

Simply put, moonshine represented life or death to these humble farm families for whom survival of the fittest was a daily way of life in the rugged enclaves they inhabited far from urban centers.

The law also required that stills be registered, as well as productions recorded and the products labeled. The government's goal was threefold: recoup the war

In 1785, Franklin County, Virginia, was founded in the Roanoke region of the Blue Ridge foothills. Named in honor of Ben Franklin and known as the Land of 60,000 Springs, Franklin County's first residents—mostly Scots-Irish immigrants—almost immediately started whipping up batches of moonshine. Locations like Shooting Creek and Rennet Bag Creek were popular havens for moonshiners. Their efforts would endure and make the area famous by one day gaining Franklin County the distinction of being the "Moonshine Capital of the World."

Wilkes County, North Carolina, and Dawsonville, Georgia, are both also known as the "Moonshine Capital of the World."

debt, create a steady flow of income to fund the new country, and keep tabs on distillers—namely the moonshiners—for easy surveillance.

Big brother government had quickly risen and was relentless in exerting its perceived powers of supremacy. This emerging dynamic ignited the ongoing debate over an invasive federal government versus states' rights, as well as big business versus small business.

Business-savvy farmers, who understood they could enhance their income by turning their excess corn and other grains—such as wheat, barley, and rye—into liquid gold, soon found themselves under the intense scrutiny of the U.S. government. They weren't keen on this tug-of-war between big government and the little guy.

Suddenly, the system of British taxes and oppression they had recently helped to defeat seemed reincarnated with a vengeance.

No. 126 "Moonshine Still Captured by Revenue Officers on Williams River, W.Va

To moonshiners, the new freedoms achieved on the back of their sacrifices on the battlefield were once more under attack. And this time, from the inside.

With unwavering fortitude and resolve, moonshiners responded by ignoring these new taxes while continuing to secretly do what they did best: make their white lightning in forests, caves, and along fresh-water streams. The stage was then set for a showdown of epic proportions.

Ahead was a period that would further define a young nation navigating its way into an uncertain future. It would become one more notch on the belts of moonshiners, signifying that the greed and blunt-force coercion of government authority was no match for their passion, loyalty, and determination.

The rebel spirit of the moonshiners would not back down.

Sometimes, moonshiners were able to sway revenuers to the dark side by bribing them to look the other way. These payoffs were known as Granny Fees.

The Whiskey Tax had instantly created a Them-Versus-Us nation between government and citizens—especially tax-evading moonshiners. The moonshine itself wasn't illegal, but the fact that the distillers refused to pay taxes based on principle was.

The government soon hired inspectors—called revenuers, or gaugers—to spy on and track down moonshiners, slapping them with fines and hauling them in for prosecution. Often, the moonshiners had to travel to the original U.S. capital city of Philadelphia for trial, at debilitating personal expense.

The interactions between revenuers and moonshiners turned farms and forests into the new battlefields of the day, resulting in beatings, whippings, gunfights, effigy burnings, and a form of true colonial justice: tarring and feathering. Often, revenuers would be stripped to the waist, covered in tar (likely pine tar as opposed to today's petroleum tar), and then doused or rolled in feathers.

The U.S. government quickly learned the fury of scorned moonshiners. These tough men and women still had many tricks left up their sleeves, and they weren't going down without a good fight. In July 1794, Pittsburgh, Pennsylvania, became ground zero for the growing outrage over federal taxes on alcohol production. On July 16 of that year, nearly five hundred armed protestors, led by Captain James McFarlane, avenged the Whiskey Tax by invading Inspector of Revenue John Neville's western Pennsylvania Bower Hill mansion. Neville was unharmed, but his home was pillaged and outbuildings burned. McFarlene was killed in the siege, only to become a rebel martyr in the moonshiners cause for freedom.

A few weeks later, on August 1, around seven thousand Pennsylvanians—rebel moonshiners known as the "Whiskey Boys," some outfitted in uniforms and others in Native American garb; hailing mostly from Fayette, Washington, Westmoreland, and Allegheny Counties—gathered at Braddock's Field along the Monongahela River, a place then known as Whiskey Point. Organized by lawyer David Bradford, the moonshiners discussed separating from the United States They even created a new flag of independence.

Rye Whiskey

Monongahela rye whiskey was both party starter and currency in western Pennsylvania at this time. It was used to pay workers and to barter for merchandise like salt, building supplies, and weapons.

Treasury Secretary Alexander Hamilton had zero sympathy for the plight of defiant moonshiners. To him, they were thugs.

In a 1792 letter to his boss, President George Washington, Hamilton made a recommendation regarding those who resisted the Whiskey Tax: "My present clear conviction is, that it is indispensable, if competent evidence can be obtained, to exert the full force of the law against the offenders." Moonshiners were clearly in his sights early on, as were the larger group of whiskey rebels in western Pennsylvania.

In a symbolic gesture of defiance, Whiskey Rebels erected Liberty Poles, which were often tall wooden poles topped with a liberty cap.

In the wake of the protest at Braddock's Field, Hamilton demonstrated how fiercely he detested rebellious moonshiners, calling them treasonous, "plotters of mischief," "caballers, intriguers, and demagogues." Assuming the penname "Tully," he wrote four editorials in the Philadelphia newspaper *Dunlap and Claypoole's American Daily Advertiser*. Hamilton utilized the letters to specifically slam the rebel-moonshiners in Pennsylvania.

In his first letter, dated August 23, 1794, Hamilton wrote, "It has from the first establishment of your present constitution been predicted, that every occasion of serious embarrassment which should occur in the affairs of the government—every misfortune which it should experience, whether produced from its own faults or mistakes, or from other causes, would be the signal of an attempt to overthrow it, or to lay the foundation of its overthrow, by defeating the exercise of constitutional and necessary authorities. The disturbances which have recently broken out in the western counties of Pennsylvania furnish an occasion of this sort."

Hamilton's words were every bit as sharp and targeted as any bullets blasted in revolution. Boundary lines were set, enemies scoped in.

"But the four western counties of Pennsylvania, undertake to rejudge and reverse your decrees," Hamilton wrote in his second Tully letter, published on August 26, 1794. "You have said, 'The Congress *shall have power* to lay *Excises*.' They say, 'The Congress *shall not have* this power.' Or what is equivalent—they shall not exercise it:—for a *power* that may not be exercised is a nullity. Your Representatives have said, and four times repeated it, 'an excise on distilled spirits *shall* be collected.' They say it *shall not* be collected."

Hamilton was so driven in his mission that he also went above President Washington's head and crafted a presidential proclamation vilifying the moonshiners.

The combative secretary of the treasury lobbied for swift and immediate use of military force against these whiskey rebels. President George Washington instead sought first to negotiate with them, albeit to little avail as passions on both sides now boiled over all attempts at reason and compromise.

Washington soon realized he had no choice but to strong-arm the moonshiners. He organized a militia force of some thirteen thousand troops—led by Hamilton and Virginia governor Henry Lee (father of future Confederate general Robert E. Lee)—from various states, such as Pennsylvania, Virginia, Maryland, and New Jersey. Their sole mission was to disperse the moonshiners in western Pennsylvania and show them who was boss.

This move was a success, effectively ending the period that has become immortalized as the Whiskey Rebellion—the first major test pitting the U.S. government against the people it was established to represent and serve. The government prevailed this time and the excise taxes on alcohol remained intact, for the time being. This period also launched the makings of a two-party system of politics in the United States. The Hamilton-led Federalists supported increased federal authority and the Whiskey Tax; Thomas Jefferson's Democratic-Republican Party opposed it. (Jefferson would repeal the excise tax on whiskey in 1802, during his presidency.)

In his January 1, 1795, "National Thanksgiving Proclamation," President Washington alluded to his victory over moonshiners, heralding the "reasonable control which has been given to a spirit of disorder in the suppression of the late insurrection."

No doubt, moonshiners begged to differ. They were far from giving up. One lost battle does not a moonshine war make. They knew the searing brand of insurrection was theirs to forever bear. And bear it they did, proudly and for all to see. Surrender was not in their vocabulary.

The art of moonshining continued. Moonshiners were even more emboldened. Uneducated as they may have been, they possessed a grassroots wisdom that cannot be learned from any teacher, book, or classroom. They innately understood that something far more important than taxes or warfare was at stake here: freedom *and* fun.

Never quitters, moonshiners doubled down. They headed deeper into the hollows, caves, and lush forests, mostly in the South, but also outward into the expanding frontier. They knew they still had a lot of history to blaze and many more jugs of XXX to distill.

The mission of the moonshiners had only just begun.

Moonshiners Hall of Fame

Nancy the Moonshiner

During the late 1880s, an eccentric Warren County, New Jersey, resident named Nancy became one of the first female moonshiners. She established herself as an astute businesswoman who outsmarted the law while stealing apples from a nearby orchard to make her hard apple cider called Jersey Lightning or what was also called Apple Jack.

CHAPTER 4

By the Light of the Silvery Moon

As the nineteenth century dawned on the U.S., moonshining—along with every moonshiner's intensifying distrust of authority—continued across places like Pennsylvania, Virginia, Kentucky, West Virginia, Georgia, Tennessee, and the Carolinas. The moonshine industry and its earliest entrepreneurs were now challenged to find ever new and covert ways to produce and distribute their XXX to very thirsty and faithful customers.

In 1800, Founding Father and leader of the new Democratic-Republican Party (eventually the Republican Party), Vice President Thomas Jefferson—a connoisseur of wine and a staunch opponent of Alexander Hamilton's

Federalist Party beliefs—ran for president on the platform promise to repeal the Whiskey Tax of 1791 if elected. He was a firm believer in the rights of the individual. His Democratic-Republican platform—especially popular in the rural South (aka, moonshine country)—prevailed, signaling the waning influence of the Federalist Party.

After Jefferson became the third president of the United States, he upheld his promise. The ears of moonshiners surely perked up as Jefferson harkened so eloquently in his inaugural address: "Let us restore to social intercourse that harmony and affection without which liberty and even life itself are but dreary things."

In 1802, President Jefferson abolished the Whiskey Tax. Jugs of 'shine were lifted in victory once more. Cheers echoed from hollow to hollow, hamlet to hamlet: *Justice at last!*

This was a defining moment when the citizens' understanding of their power to rock the vote to effect change was realized.

Jefferson may well have had the unyielding perseverance of moonshiners in mind years earlier when he wrote: "The tree of liberty must be refreshed from time to time with the blood of patriots and tyrants." For moonshiners, the tree of

liberty and progress was always tall and gnarly, with many branches of opportunity extending north, south, east, and west.

As moonshiners distilled their way full steam ahead into this new century, there were approximately fourteen thousand active stills in the United States, producing 8.6 million gallons of whiskey.

For the sixty years that followed—except for a brief period from 1813 to 1817 during the War of 1812 when re-enforcement of alcohol taxes helped fund the war—moonshiners were granted a reprieve. They more or less were free to produce their whiskey in peace.

Then came the American Civil War from 1861 to 1865.

And with it, history repeated itself brutally like a nightmare flashback for moonshiners. Law-abiding distillers and moonshiners alike—now producing nearly ninety million gallons of whiskey a year—were once again planted firmly in the cross-hairs of the U.S. government.

The government again instituted a stiff tax on alcohol, while also making all untaxed and unregulated liquor illegal.

The Revenue Act of 1861, signed into law by President Abraham Lincoln, established the country's first income tax, which was meant to help fund the Union Army. This was followed by a more

During this time, the temperance movement continued to grow. In the early 1800s, a preacher named Lyman Beecher became a leading advocate for the movement, which included his *Six Sermons on Intemperance*. In Sermon 1: "The Nature and Occasions of Intemperance," he declared: "No sin has fewer apologies than intemperance."

Exemplars of this tenacious attitude, from 1863 to 1891 along the Tug Fork area of the Big Sandy River, the Hatfield clan of West Virginia and the McCoy clan of Kentucky—both of which knew their way around a moonshine still—ignited the most famous family feud in American history. Theirs was a story of betrayal and bloodshed, land disputes and a stolen pig, a New Year's massacre, and even a *Romeo and Juliet*-style romance. While their story became legend for the ages, there was one other valuable piece of their heritage that would also survive: patriarch Devil Anse Hatfield's original recipe for moonshine. Little did the two families know then that this white lightning in a jug would become an ultimate olive branch more than a century later.

M expansive bill—the Revenue Act of 1862, which eliminated the income tax provision in favor of a progressive tax scale and also established the Internal Revenue Service as a bureau of the U.S. Department of the Treasury. These new laws included the strictest taxes yet on alcohol. In 1862, the alcohol tax was twenty-cents per gallon. By 1864, the tax rose to two dollars per gallon. It became clear to moonshiners that the sky was the limit where taxes and government control were concerned.

Resistance by moonshiners against the government seemed futile, coming at the cost of prosecution and the government seizing personal assets. However, the U.S. government still didn't comprehend just who they were dealing with when it came to moonshiners. These were resilient, wise, seasoned men and women who had already trudged through the worst of times.

Muzzled obedience and blind loyalty meant nothing

to moonshiners. To the contrary, principle and victory were everything.

Alas, moonshiners at-large still had their dues to pay. During his stint as commissioner of internal revenue at the IRS from 1876 to 1883, Green Berry Raum—a former Union Army brigadier general—created a police agency out of the tax collectors. One of their sole missions: bring moonshiners to justice.

While campaigning on an anti-revenue platform in 1876, North Carolina senator Zebulon Vance labeled revenuers as "red-legged grasshoppers."

IRS agents were ferocious in their hot pursuit of illegal moonshine operations. They often relied on intel from informants, such as disapproving townsfolk and even a moonshiner's own competitors, in what became a dog-eat-dog race to the finish line.

Over the course of the next twenty years, the numerous stake-outs, stand-offs, ambushes, raids, and shootouts resulted in the destruction of more than five thousand of the nearly fifteen thousand stills in operation and more than eight thousand moonshine-related arrests. For moonshiners, this was more than just an injustice, it was an outrageous infringement on their culture and way of life.

One surefire way revenuers had for decommissioning a still was to hack holes in it with axes and other instruments. Another, more dramatic, method for demolishing a moonshine operation was dynamite. They also turned over barrels of mash, flooding the countryside with white lightning.

These fierce battles— during which some moonshiners were even in cahoots with local law enforcement to preserve their way of life—often resulted in fellow townspeople being threatened to not reveal the location of stills, and IRS agents being brutalized and their families threatened.

In the 1870s, one of the most famous crackdowns on moonshine operations—known as the Whiskey Ring—involved a group of moonshiners and the government agents and politicians they had bribed in cities like St. Louis, Chicago, Milwaukee, Peoria, Cincinnati, and New Orleans. Under the determined leadership of Secretary of the Treasury Benjamin Bristow, in May 1875, undercover agents infiltrated the circle of perpetrators and arrested them.

As the 1900s approached, such raucous moonshiner tactics added fuel to the fiery agenda of temperance activists—dominated by women, evangelicals, and journalists. As their anti-booze movement gained momentum, they became increasingly determined to stomp out the evils of alcohol and ban it altogether.

These teetotalers would soon relish in the historic victory they sought, while moonshiners continued to find themselves embroiled in the tumultuous fight for their lives, principles, and livelihoods. But like many before them, the temperance movement underestimated moonshiners. In sharpening their judgmental teeth on the cusp of a new century, temperance activists would also come to learn that moonshiners were a rock-solid bunch of patriot-entrepreneurs who never gave up, come hell or firewater.

During the latter half of the nineteenth century, Southern moonshiners were mostly concentrated in western North Carolina, western South Carolina, eastern Tennessee, northern Georgia, and the Blue Ridge Mountains.

There was one more miscalculation temperance activists would make. Moonshiners would prove without a doubt the human inclination that when people are told they can't have something, that only makes them want it all the more.

Moonshiners Hall of Fame

Amos Owens

Prior to the Civil War, Amos Owens began his career as a distiller on Cherry Mountain in Rutherford County, North Carolina. Despite run-ins with the revenuers—whom he called "red-legged grasshoppers" and to whom he offered a few swigs when they came to arrest him—and even stints in jail, he became a famous moonshiner. His legendary creation was Cherry Bounce: a medley of corn whiskey, homegrown cherries, and honey, which made him a household name as far away as the Mississippi River.

A veteran of the Confederate Army during the Civil War, Amos—also known as the "Cherry Bounce King"—was beloved for the huge parties he threw at his mountain retreat, where the great food and his cherry moonshine flowed freely.

CHAPTER 5
Temperance Tantrum

Following the groundbreaking publication of Benjamin Rush's *An Inquiry into the Effects of Ardent Spirits upon the Human Body and Mind* in 1784, the grip of the temperance movement squeezed ever tighter in the century and a half that followed, especially in the cradle of moonshine country.

Moonshiners found themselves in the eye of this hurricane of staunch teetotalers, who claimed God and morality were on their side. But one of the things moonshiners were good at was spotting an opportunity, and the temperance crowd presented a big one.

Temperance associations and societies were started in cities and small rural towns. They aggressively tugged at the hearts and minds of citizens in an attempt to squire them to their side. They even targeted children, planting their anti-alcohol agenda in school textbooks with the hope of recruiting future temperance advocates and voters.

As the temperance movement picked up steam, society was divided into two groups: the "Wets"—moonshiners among them, who supported a society where folks were free to imbibe to their heart's content—and the "Drys," who advocated for restrictions and all-out bans on liquor consumption.

In 1826, the American Temperance Society was founded. Within a decade, the organization would boast nearly ten thousand local chapters and well over a million members nationwide. Each member was required to embrace a solemn pledge to give up alcohol.

Like moonshiners, the temperance crowd was also a crafty bunch, especially when it came to public relations. Their movement heralded the birth of a new theatrical genre that doubled

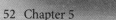

as propaganda. The hottest tickets around were to performances of such 1841 temperance plays as Douglas Jerrold's *Fifteen Years of a Drunkard's Life* and W.H. Smith's *The Drunkard*.

The media outreach for the movement included the circulation of eighteen journals specifically dedicated to promoting temperance. The National Temperance Society and Publishing House, founded in 1865, published more than a billion pages of pro-temperance propaganda for adults and children during the next several decades. Clearly, this literature was not found in any moonshiner's private library.

The year 1869 saw the formation of a political party called the Prohibition Party—the platform of which was obvious—under the leadership of its first chairman, a preacher and publisher named John Russell. Russell was also the Prohibition Party's vice presidential candidate in 1872

Circa 1846, Nathaniel Currier of Currier & Ives fame created a legendary lithograph titled *The Drunkards Progress: From the First Glass to the Grave.* The piece depicts a weeping woman and child over which arches a half circle of men, charting the nine ominous steps of demise via alcohol:

1. A glass with a Friend.
2. A glass to keep the cold out.
3. A glass too much.
4. Drunk and riotous.
5. The summit attained. Jolly Companions. A confirmed Drunkard.
6. Poverty and Disease.
7. Forsaken by Friends.
8. Desperation and crime.
9. Death by suicide.

This was one of thirty prints Currier & Ives produced about the temperance movement.

when he ran with co-founder James Black. While they lost, and surely didn't receive a single moonshiner's vote, their efforts helped to solidify the tradition of third parties and candidates as alternatives on the national political scene. Furthermore, Russell's *Peninsular Herald* in Detroit was the country's first newspaper dedicated to the cause of prohibition.

OLD COMPANY "B" AT WILLIAMSON COURTHOUSE DURING YEAR OF 1921 OR 1922. THIS PICTURE IS THE PROPERTY OF SAM TAYLOR, THE FIRST MAN TO ENLIST IN THE D.P.S.

The temperance activists railed against the saloon culture of the day when bars and taverns were the hubs of a community's activity, especially for the male citizens. Activists pointed the finger of blame squarely at alcohol—particularly high-proof spirits like moonshine and other whiskey—for causing an increase in the abuse of women and children, ending marriages, crushing family life, inciting crime and violence, and waning productivity in the workplace. While their concerns were not untrue, these mostly religious- and female-populated protest groups had a steep hill to climb if they wanted to come between a citizen and his booze, *and* a moonshiner and his still.

Following the Civil War, the Women's Christian Temperance Union was founded in 1874 and named reformer Annie Wittenmyer as its first president. The organization's goal was to use abstinence and faith to create a "sober and pure world." The hundreds of thousands of members who were banded together in state chapters across the country bought into this credo lock, stock, and barrel.

Another moonshine milestone occurred around this time when the term "bootlegger" was coined in the 1880s in the American Midwest. It originally described men who secretly concealed bottles of moonshine in their boots to use when trading with Native Americans. Eventually, the term expanded to include not only the sellers of moonshine but also was used synonymously for moonshiner and moonshine runner.

The bell-bottom pants that would become popular fashion staples almost a century later were also known as bootleg pants, a nice subtle allusion to moonshine history.

In 1893, American Temperance University opened in the dry town of Harriman, Tennessee. And in towns everywhere, temperance fountains were erected in public places to provide drinking water as an alternative to alcohol. Surely the unschooled moonshiners of the day scoffed at both. Theirs was a hands-on education filtered down through generations, not classrooms. And for them, water was most refreshing when distilled together with corn, yeast, and other grains.

One of the most influential temperance groups to emerge was the Anti-Saloon League, founded by Reverend Howard Hyde Russell in 1893. Its motto: "the Church in action against the saloon." Charging into the twentieth century, the Anti-Saloon League quickly supplanted

Beginning in the 1890s, cartoonist Frank Beard created some of the most enduring images that became representative of the temperance movement in the late nineteenth century. His illustrations depicted greedy and cunning bar owners, corrupt authorities, sloppy drunks, and children whom temperance activists believed were vulnerable to the temptations of alcohol. One illustration titled *Fifteen Minutes with the Barkeeper* depicts the barkeeper quickly morphing from a drinker's friend into a devilish rogue. Likewise, Beard's *Rescued* portrays an angel rescuing an innocent child from a seedy saloon.

other temperance organizations to become the leading national force in the push for Prohibition.

And one of the movement's boldest activists was six-foot-tall, 180-pound Carrie Nation, who declared, "[I am] a bulldog running along at the feet of Jesus, barking at what he doesn't like!" Radical to the core, Nation was propelled onward by what she deemed to be a divine calling to abolish the evils of alcohol. Few ever got in her way as she brandished a trademark hatchet with which she attacked taverns and other places where alcohol was served. During these "hatchetations" as she called them, Nation sang hymns and prayers, and chastised drinkers, as she demolished bottles of booze and interiors of saloons.

Under mounting pressure from temperance groups and activists like Nation, county after county, and town after town chose to become dry communities. As bars and even licensed distilleries— that supplied larger cities, and factory and coal towns—closed, and local store shelves emptied the last of their liquor supplies, back-hill moonshiners soon championed another art form: supply and demand.

If a thirsty citizen looking for a little buzz couldn't get it in town, he simply sought out his friendly neighborhood moonshiner, who was more than willing to hook him up. For moonshiners, white lightning was still a mode of survival. Corn as liquid gold was still easier to transport by horse and wagon over craggy back roads and meant more money in a farmer's pocket. So, while temperance activists and authorities took many moonshine stills out of commission, moonshiners trudged ahead and set more into motion.

In the midst of this Progressive Era swarming with judgment and temperance activists, moonshiners grinned ear to ear. With each crackdown, sermon, pamphlet, and ban waged against moonshine and liquor in general, the demand for their XXX rose. After all, moonshining was a full-fledged industry now, comprising a web of skilled artisans; suppliers and manufacturers for ingredients and containers; bootleggers and runners delivering the white lightning to stores, bars, railroad stops, and even homes; and retailers selling the moonshine. Not to mention the authorities whom the moonshiners kept in business and on their toes 24/7.

Regardless of any disruption or setback within the moonshine industry, by either temperance activists or the authorities, there was always one indomitable constant that remained strong as the 1910s and 1920s loomed just ahead: the moonshiners themselves, who weren't going anywhere!

Moonshiners Hall of Fame

Simmie Free

Quitting elementary school, Simmie Free helped his Scotsman father make moonshine in Rabun County, Georgia, where he would eventually become one of the region's most notable moonshiners. Today, Dawsonville Distillery in Dawsonville, Georgia—home to the Moonshine Festival—uses an heirloom moonshine recipe that Simmie used.

Josephine Doody

Known as the "Bootleg Lady of Glacier National Park," Josephine Doody was a dance-hall gal who became one of the region's most celebrated moonshiners. Working from her ranch near McCarthyville, Josephine maintained numerous stills and supplied her hooch to many railroaders on the Great Northern Railway line at Marias Pass.

CHAPTER 6

The First Golden Age of Moonshiners, 1920 to 1933

"Section 1. After one year from the ratification of this article the manufacture, sale, or transportation of intoxicating liquors within, the importation thereof into, or the exportation thereof from the United States and all the territory subject to the jurisdiction thereof for beverage purposes is hereby prohibited."

The Eighteenth Amendment of the U.S. Constitution was ratified on January 16, 1919, and went into effect on January 16, 1920.

"Prohibition"—one of the dirtiest words ever uttered in American history, at least to everyone who enjoyed a swig of white lightning or other spirits every now and then. But to the dry crusaders in government and across the nation, they believed this was the answer to many problems of the day. In their minds: Eliminate alcohol, and then issues like crime, alcoholism, lethargic workers, and domestic abuse would also decline. Likewise, they hoped that instead of spending money on booze, citizens would now funnel their cash to other businesses in town—both retail and entertainment, creating an economic resurgence.

Scofflaw: Prohibition-era term used for folks who defied the law and continued to drink illegally.

The National Prohibition Act—the brainchild of Anti-Saloon League lobbyist Wayne Wheeler—was also passed by the U.S. Congress in October 1919 and went into effect on February 1, 1920. It was enacted to further ensure the Eighteenth Amendment and Prohibition reigned supreme as the law of the land.

Nicknamed the Volstead Act after chairman of the House Judiciary Committee and staunch Prohibitionist Andrew Volstead, this Act further validated the Eighteenth Amendment and laid out which "intoxicating liquors" were to be banned, as well as the federal-enforcement guidelines (i.e., stiff fines and penalties) for offenders. While Democrat president Woodrow Wilson vetoed the bill, he was overridden by the dry crusaders within the U.S. Congress and more informally by those in society, who had finally achieved the goal set in motion by their temperance ancestors almost a century and a half earlier.

The Volstead Act's rebuke of moonshiners and other alcohol manufacturers, and their thirsty patrons, was sharp: "No person shall on or after the date when the eighteenth amendment to the Constitution of the United States goes into effect, manufacture, sell, barter, transport, import, export, deliver, furnish or possess any intoxicating liquor except as authorized in this Act, and all the provisions of this Act shall be liberally construed to the end that the use of intoxicating liquor as a beverage may be prevented."

The only exemptions were the use of alcohol for medicinal purposes, which meant alcohol prescribed by a doctor and sold by a licensed pharmacy, and for religious reasons, which meant mostly church wine. Neither of these exceptions formally included

moonshine, though many a moonshiner would certainly have added his two cents in confirming the benefits of white lightning on body *and* spirit! Being that Americans are an enterprising lot, it wasn't coincidental in light of these exemptions, the number of licensed pharmacies and folks taking ill suddenly grew and attendance at church spiked.

Prohibition

Prohibition highlighted tensions between social classes. Prior to the ban, the wealthy stockpiled booze as provisions for surviving the long dry spell. The working class and poor didn't have the luxury of doing this, but were as thirsty as the next guy when Prohibition hit.

From their perches in the hills, hollows, and along the streams of Appalachia and beyond, moonshiners simply sat back and laughed at this latest boondoggle, albeit the crowning jewel in the temperance movement. If the growing anti-booze campaign during the last several decades—which saw whole states, regions, and towns go dry while demand for moonshine actually increased—had turned them into folk heroes, then Prohibition was about to now christen moonshiners as bona fide super heroes.

The infrastructure of moonshine—from copper pot still to transportation to final destination—was firmly in place in Appalachia and elsewhere, and more than ready for this great boom across the country. Soon, the number of moonshine stills tripled, then quadrupled. Profits skyrocketed. Moonshiners had never been busier, or richer. They had stood their ground against government interference many times before, so this was nothing new. When opportunity knocked, these revolutionaries always answered the call.

Batches of white lightning flowing from down-home places like Rocky Mount in Franklin County, Virginia; Dawson, Gilmer, Pickens, and Lumpkin Counties in Georgia; Wilkes County and Buffalo City in North Carolina; Cocke County, Tennessee; Nelson County, Kentucky; Clay County, Florida; and New Straitsville, Ohio, would all help solidify moonshine's iconic status on the American scene during this time.

During Prohibition, nip joints and shot houses started popping up around the South, often in people's homes or on farms. These were locations where thirsty lower- and middle-class revelers could privately enjoy moonshine.

Whereas previously moonshiners had supplied more of a local and regional customer base, now urban bars and clubs from coast to coast that had once purchased alcohol legally were added to their delivery routes. Prohibition instantly ignited the advent of the speakeasy—underground establishments, bustling with locals,

socialites, industry barons, celebrities, and gangsters, *and* eternal fountains of outlawed booze.

Some of the most famous Prohibition-era speakeasies included:

- Chumley's, founded by Leland Stanford Chumley in Greenwich Village in 1922

- Dil Pickle Club, founded by Wobbly Jack Jones in Chicago in 1917

- Gallagher's Steakhouse, founded by Helen Gallagher in Manhattan in 1927

- Krazy Kat Club, founded by Cleon Throckmorton in Washington, D.C. in early 1900s

The king of this scene was notorious mobster Al Capone. His approach was simple supply and demand, giving folks what they wanted while snatching his slice of the American dream. "This American system of ours, call it Americanism, call it what you will, gives each of us a great opportunity if we only seize it with both hands and make the most of it," Capone touted.

While Capone left a trail of violence, bloodshed, corruption, racketeering, and moonshine in his wake, he did so with a twisted sense of humor. He once said, "When I sell liquor, it's called bootlegging; when my patrons serve it on Lake Shore Drive, it's called hospitality." Touché.

Cities like Capone's Chicago, New York, Atlanta, and San Francisco became hubs for thousands of speakeasies. And more and more moonshine production started up in places like Brooklyn. The black market for this high-octane contraband was never so bright and glittery.

Simultaneously, Prohibition became the first Golden Age for both moonshiners and mobsters. Like the mountain moonshine operations from the start, speakeasies were the newest altars at which these boozy entrepreneurs and their gangs preached their own brand of fun and mischief, relished in their Midas touch, and served the parched.

Organized crime bosses—gangsters and mobsters, like the Chicago Outfit led by Capone—ran most of the speakeasies where white lightning lit up the room day and night. To avert the law, patrons often had to recite passwords, use secret knocks, or show membership cards, as well as enter and exit through secret passages. Adding to the aura of the Roaring Twenties, it was well worth the cost of admission to enjoy these clandestine places where reality was checked at the door and one could indulge in the best jazz, hooch, and fashions of the day.

> Bathtub gin referred to poor quality spirits, often made in a bathtub to allude detection. While not distilled, bathtub gin was moonshine all the same. In speakeasies, bathtub gin and other moonshine starred in such cocktails as Bee's Knees, Highball, Tuxedo #2, Dubonnet Cocktail, Sidecar, Southside, Old Fashioned, and French 75.

Amid the glitz and glamour of these swanky juice joints, moonshine cocktails were paired with dolled-up women in bobbed cuts and flapper dresses—adorned with feathers, sequins, beads, fringe, fur, sparkly jewels—and their dapper Dans with slicked hair and sharp suits with whom they rocked the night away in a smoky haze of saxophones, trumpets, and percussion. From the beginning, fun had always been moonshine's calling card, so the illicit liquor guzzled in speakeasies only fueled the sheer abandonment.

Within every speakeasy, all measures were taken to one: avoid a raid by the Feds, and two: have a blast. These were the places to see and be seen.

And even under the weight of the Wall Street Crash of 1929 and the early years of the Great Depression, while many Americans suffered, moonshiners and mobsters prospered and partied. These renegades were quickly besting the U.S. government and the flawed hopes of Prohibition.

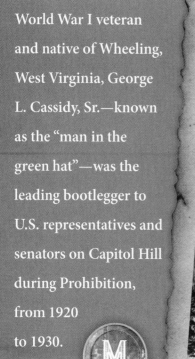

World War I veteran and native of Wheeling, West Virginia, George L. Cassidy, Sr.—known as the "man in the green hat"—was the leading bootlegger to U.S. representatives and senators on Capitol Hill during Prohibition, from 1920 to 1930.

However, all that glitters is not gold. Because of the enormous demand for moonshine from back-road America to city avenues, the quality of the finished product began to suffer. The lure of easy profits led some new and also established moonshiners to skimp on using the purest ingredients and production methods. Quantity soon vanquished quality.

The resulting moonshine—often referred to as "mean whiskey" or "jake" (when distilled with high-octane Jamaican ginger)—left in its wake blindness, paralysis, organ failure, nerve damage, and thousands of deaths. Drinkers imbibing this substandard moonshine often suffered from jake leg syndrome—their legs and feet would become partially or fully paralyzed.

By cutting corners, and sometimes in an attempt to add an extra kick to their white lightning, some moonshiners inadvertently contaminated their recipe with chemicals. This included industrial alcohol that the government purposely tainted to—albeit unsuccessfully—prevent it from being stolen and used to make moonshine, as well as methanol (used in denatured alcohol), battery acid, creosote, lye, paint thinner, manure, bleach, rubbing alcohol, embalming fluid, and even lead that resulted from some moonshiners using car radiators to manufacture their generic 'shine. In fact, a lot of moonshine during this period was downright poisonous.

Woody Gutherie famously wrote a song titled "Jake Walk Blues," which was released by the Allen Brothers in 1930.

Many other Prohibition-era songs also mention jake, including "Jake Bottle Blues" (1930); "Got the Jake Leg Too" (1930); "Jake Leg Rag" (1930); "Alcohol and Jake Blues" (1930); and "Jake Walk Pappa" (1933).

Just as the moonshiners worked tirelessly, the revenuers hot on their trail were as busy as ever, too. With the passage of the Eighteenth Amendment, the Bureau of Prohibition was also established to enforce the tenets of the Volstead Act. The Bureau's main mission: stop the selling and consumption of alcohol. These were the folks taxed with raiding speakeasies and moonshine operations, and cracking the related crime rings wide open.

The most famous of these Prohibition agents—also known as G-men—was Eliot Ness and his team known as the Untouchables. Their main focus at this time was to bring down Al Capone and his empire.

"Unquestionably, it was going to be highly dangerous," Ness said of his assignment. "Yet I felt it was quite natural to jump at the task. After all, if you don't like action and excitement, you don't go into police work. And, what the hell, I figured, nobody lives forever!"

Eliot Ness's autobiography *The Untouchables* (written with Oscar Fraley) inspired the popular television crime series of the same name that aired from 1959 to 1963.

These lawmen across the board carefully stalked moonshiners and bootleggers who were transporting their brew in both cities and in the countryside. During raids on speakeasies and rural moonshine operations, they made arrests and seized everything from stills, mules, and wagons to cars, trucks, and the moonshine itself.

But the Prohibition enforcers often fell prey to the temptations of supplementing meager salaries with generous bribes to look the other way. This was merely one more crack in the good intentions of an amendment that was proving itself to be tarnished beyond repair.

Especially throughout Appalachia, many of the cat-and-mouse encounters resulted in high-speed chases along old dirt roads. The bootleggers—either working with moonshiners or sometimes they were the moonshiners themselves pulling double duty—did their best to leave the revenuers spinning out in a cloud of dust. Long a harbinger of cultural change and invention, the moonshine industry's fast cars and whiskey in Mason jars would soon distill pure magic once again by launching the origin of an American institution: stockcar racing and NASCAR.

Alas, Prohibition—what President Herbert Hoover coined in 1928 as a "great social and economic experiment, noble in motive and far-reaching in purpose"—quickly proved itself to be a failed endeavor on many levels. To the contrary of what dry crusaders had hoped and predicted, bribed authorities fostered even more corruption; alcoholism increased; violence and crime became rampant; and the economic impact included a decrease in consumerism and the loss of thousands of jobs. And the spoiled cherry on top for the U.S. government: No legal alcohol sales meant no excise tax revenues.

Backwoods

Backwoods moonshiners would sometimes outsmart revenuers on foot by crafting and wearing cow shoes, which consisted of wooden blocks carved to look like hooves and attached to the bottom of shoes. While footprints in the fields and woods raised suspicion and created an easy trail for agents to follow to stills, hoofprints did not.

Songwriter Lowe Stokes immortalized this washout in his 1930 hit song "Prohibition Is a Failure."

Much like in 1800 when Thomas Jefferson ran for president on a platform promise to repeal the Whiskey Tax of 1791, Democrat candidate Franklin D. Roosevelt ran for president in 1932 on the platform promise to repeal Prohibition.

In an August 27 campaign address in Sea Girt, New Jersey, Roosevelt said: "The methods adopted since the World War with the purpose of achieving a greater temperance by the forcing of Prohibition have been accompanied in most parts of the country by complete and tragic failure. I need not point out to you that general encouragement of lawlessness has resulted; that corruption, hypocrisy, crime and disorder have emerged, and that instead of restricting, we have extended the spread of intemperance. This failure has come for this very good reason: we have depended too largely upon the power of governmental action instead of recognizing that the authority of the home and that of the churches in these matters is the fundamental force on which we must build."

And like President Jefferson in 1801, on December 5, 1933, the newly elected President Roosevelt made good on his promise. The Twenty-First Amendment to the U.S. Constitution finally brought the red curtain down on Prohibition.

Section 1 of the Amendment simply read: "The eighteenth article of amendment to the Constitution of the United States is hereby repealed."

Once more, cheers and toasts rang out across the nation. Citizens were again free to imbibe publicly.

And moonshiners were officially canonized in the history books.

In 1935, the Great Moonshine Conspiracy parlayed itself into the Moonshine Trial of the Century in Franklin County, Virginia. Throughout the later years of Prohibition until 1935, Franklin County officials—helmed by the sheriff—and moonshiners became entangled in a boozy and very profitable web of bribes referred to as protection fees and extortion that would eventually go up in the flames of a federal investigation and dozens of indictments. And the murder of a key witness. The elaborate moonshine operation had cost the U.S. government $5.5 million in whiskey excise taxes. The ten-week trial, which included star defendants and more than two hundred witnesses, resulted in numerous convictions and immortalized Franklin County in the history of moonshine.

Moonshiners Hall of Fame

Joshua Percy Flowers

From his expansive farm in Johnston County, North Carolina, businessman Percy Flowers became the biggest moonshine producer in North Carolina's history during the middle of the twentieth century. He was dubbed "King of the Moonshiners" by the *Saturday Evening Post* in 1958. At the height of his career, he was earning around $1 million a year in untaxed revenue from moonshine. A short documentary was created by D.L. Anderson about Percy titled *Mr. Percy's Run*.

CHAPTER 7

Moonshine Paves the Way for NASCAR

During Prohibition and the years following, the need for speed in meeting the demand for moonshine meant faster cars and skilled drivers. The latter were good ole boys by day and bootleggers by the light of the silvery moon. In the moonshine-running business, it was imperative that the G-man in his government-issued economy car be left behind in the dust.

The 1940 Ford Coupe was the car of choice for moonshine runners—also known as trippers, haulers, and moonrunners. It was all about the horsepower, and the Ford Coupe's flathead V8 engine, especially when supercharged or even swapped for a more powerful Cadillac engine, was perfect for the job. Plus, the car's suspension was easy to modify for heavy loads of sometimes as much as eight hundred to a thousand pounds of 'shine. Additional modifications to cylinders, engines, springs, and shocks armed these liquor cars with better maneuverability in handling the curvy, dirt roads of Appalachia at breakneck speeds.

In the early days of automobiles, moonshine was used as antifreeze by some folks to keep the water in their radiators from freezing in the winter.

Also, cars like the Ford Coupe were common at the time—as in, they were everyday stock cars, so they evaded suspicion. The simple design and dark paint jobs kept them off the G-man's radar, and the large trunks were roomy enough to hold dozens of gallons of white lightning. For greater storage, false rear seats were added to cover up the jugs of XXX—sometimes only covered with a blanket or fake upholstery; tanks of moonshine were stashed under the car's floorboards; and fake gas tanks were even installed to maximize storage. Modified brake lights and tail lights were used to throw off the authorities with the flip of a switch. And heavy-duty tires replaced regular ones for better grip and grind.

Along with the moonshine runners, the mechanics who transformed these cars became legendary themselves. Many of them would also find their skills at a premium as they wrenched their way into the future NASCAR circuit.

The final touch in pimping out a souped-up moonshine chariot was a fake license plate that could easily replace the real one for moonlit runs. Otherwise, the exteriors remained unchanged to blend in.

Other tanker cars that were popular among early moonshine runners were the Oldsmobile Rocket 88s, Chevy Coupes, and Dodge Coronets. Collectively, these vehicles gave face to the muscle car—the very flexing, virile, tough, indestructible symbol of mid-century manhood.

In a pinch, pickups were sometimes used for bootlegging. As were larger commercial trucks early on, but they proved to be too big and noisy for the covert missions.

Late night cat-and-mouse races with revenuers worked to the moonshiner's advantage. Regardless of any roadblocks or stakeouts by the authorities, the ensuing chases mostly occurred on old, twisty mountain roads that were home turf for the bootleggers. These rebels-with-a-cause knew all the main routes and hidden back roads by heart, making their escape all the easier.

One evasive maneuver used by runners was named the 180, or bootleg turn. When being chased by revenuers, a runner would spin his car 180 degrees, changing direction and waving with a smug grin as he passed the befuddled G-men now going in the opposite direction. One of the most famous bootleggers, Junior Johnson, often turned the 180 into a game of chicken, which left cowering authorities scratching their heads in a ditch wondering what just happened.

Plastic jugs full of white lightning eventually replaced the more breakable glass jars on many of these journeys because of the bumpy country roads.

Agents, however, sometimes turned the tables and caught the runners red-handed by throwing two-by-fours

embedded with nails onto the road. This was surely sweet revenge for the many times they had found themselves stuck in swamps and ditches after a disastrous run-in with bootleggers.

There was more than a little competitive ego among these bad boys with their hopped-up hotrods. They would boast and argue about who was the fastest driver and who had the best stock car. This boys-will-be-boys teasing eventually led them to duke it out against each other on racetracks worn into old fields, cow pastures, and fairgrounds across the South during the weekend.

COME SEE THE CRAZIEST DARE DEVILS ON THE ROAD, one ad beckoned.

Football

American football also has a small reference to the country's moonshine history. The bootleg play is one in which the goal is to confuse the defense by hiding the ball close to the quarterback's leg, á la the era of bootleggers hiding bottles of moonshine in their boots.

One of those daredevils was moonshine runner "Lightning" Lloyd Seay. An early star on the stock car circuit, this fearless racer's dreams came to an abrupt end though when he was shot to death by his cousin over a moonshine dispute in 1941. Proof again that while the moonshine industry offered its artisans and runners the moon and stars, it never insured a happy ending.

When promoters, many of whom were shady and crooked characters, got a hold of these bootleggers-turned-race-car-drivers and money started pouring in from ticket sales, more permanent racetracks started to be built. And once Prohibition ended and the demand for moonshine runs slowed—though several areas still banned alcohol so the bootlegging biz would never completely dry up—racing for profit became a tantalizing new outlet for this first generation of professional speed demons.

The many moonshine runners who turned their attention to racing cars included some of NASCAR's original superstars, such as Junior Johnson, Lee Petty (father of Richard Petty), Benny Parsons, the Flock brothers (Fonty, Tim, and Bob), Charlie Mincey, Curtis Turner, and Roy Hall. Also, Raymond Parks, a car owner, was a well-known bootlegger.

In a NASCAR.com article titled "NASCAR's Earliest Days Forever Connected to Bootlegging," Junior Johnson reflected on how he brought his unconventional training as a bootlegger to legitimate racetracks: "It gave me so much advantage over other people that had to train and learn how to drive."

This burgeoning new venture caught the eye of businessman and stock car racer-turned-promoter Big Bill France Sr., who knew a bonanza when he saw one. Sports history was made on December 14, 1947, when France convened a meeting of drivers, mechanics, and car owners at Daytona Beach's Streamline Hotel. The initial agenda of the meeting was to create standard rules for racing. This would also insure that drivers were protected from corrupt promoters. Then and there, the seed of an empire was planted.

In 1948, France formally founded the National Association for Stock Car Auto Racing—better known today by its multi-billion-dollar moniker, NASCAR. The winner of the first NASCAR race was Robert "Red" Byron, who drove a car owned by former moonshiner Raymond Parks and serviced by moonshine mechanic Red Vogt.

With the dawn of stock car racing and then NASCAR, the tower of legend built jug by jug by moonshiners since the 1700s soared a little higher. Every car that rounds a racetrack throughout the United States to this day—be it to the soundtrack of rubber on asphalt or concrete in places like Dover, Indianapolis, and Bristol, or the blur of revved engines on dirt tracks engulfing fans in billows of dust on a Saturday night at the likes of Hummingbird and Stateline Speedways—is another ripple fueled long ago by a uniquely American icon: moonshine.

Bill France Sr. would go on to also build Daytona International Speedway—home to the Daytona 500—in 1959 and the Talladega Speedway in 1969.

Today, NASCAR superstar Bill Elliott has his own signature brand of moonshine, which is produced by Dawsonville Distillery. Likewise, one of NASCAR's original superstars, Junior Johnson, also has his own line of white lightning called Midnight Moon Moonshine, produced by Piedmont Distillers, Inc. The NASCAR Hall of Fame has a still that was built especially for their collection by Junior.

Moonshiners Hall of Fame

Tim Smith

Outlaw turned legal moonshiner, Tim Smith is the star and a fan favorite on Discovery Channel's *Moonshiners*. A third-generation moonshiner from Climax in Pittsylvania County, Virginia, Tim launched Climax Moonshine—the "Drink of Defiance"—so he could share his homemade moonshine throughout the United States. Also serving as the town's fire chief, Tim is the ultimate inside link bridging moonshine's storied past with its invigorated renaissance today as a legitimate staple of commerce and fun.

CHAPTER 8

A Shining Star is Born

By the 1950s and 1960s, moonshiners had so far enjoyed a very productive, and profitable, twentieth century. They had helped launch NASCAR and had kept thirsty revelers well satiated during the thirteen years of Prohibition.

It was now time for them and their white lightning to take on a new role: A-lister, superstar, celebrity thirst quencher, and pop culture icon.

Moonshiners on Music Row

Moonshiners and moonshine have long been muses for songwriters and singers, who wrote such folk songs as the nineteenth century folk ballad "The Kentucky Moonshiner" and "Good Old Mountain Dew," which has two versions: one from 1928 (written by Bascom Lamar Lunsford) and one from 1935 (written by Scotty Wiseman). The 1935 version was recorded numerous times, including by Grandpa Jones and Willie Nelson. Another popular moonshine ditty is "Copper Kettle" written by Albert Frank Beddoe in 1953 and later immortalized by Joan Baez, and Bob Dylan, who also sang "Moonshiner."

Moonshine as a theme found a particularly welcoming home in Country Music over the years: Dolly Parton's "Daddy's Moonshine Still" (written by Dolly Parton); Hank Williams Jr.'s "Ballad of the Moonshine" (written by Hank Williams Jr.); Robert Mitchum's "The Ballad of Thunder Road" (written by Don Raye and Robert Mitchum as the title track for his movie *Thunder Road*); George Jones's "White Lightning" (written by J.P. Richardson—the Big Bopper—also recorded by Conway Twitty and Waylon Jennings); Osborne Brothers' "Rocky Top" (written by Felice Bryant and Boudleaux Bryant);

During the mid-twentieth century, while moonshine made its foray into the entertainment business, the authorities—still on the trail of real-life moonshiners—destroyed tens of thousands of stills throughout the South where the majority of the country's moonshine continued to be produced. By this time, revenuers had also started using planes to track down moonshiners, which forced many moonshiners to move their operations inside.

Hank Williams III's "Moonshiner's Life" (written by Hank Williams III); Florida Georgia Line's "Get Your Shine On" (written by Brian Kelley, Tyler Hubbard, Rodney Clawson, and Chris Tompkins); Jake Owen's "Apple Pie Moonshine" (written by Rodney Clawson, Chris Tompkins, Chad Kroeger, and Craig Wiseman); and Brad Paisley's album and title song "Moonshine in the Trunk" (written by Brad Paisley, Brent Anderson, Kelley Lovelace, and Chris DuBois).

Some Country Music superstars even have direct links to the legacy of white lightning. Loretta Lynn's husband and manager Doolittle Lynn had previously made a living as a moonshiner. This earned him the nickname Mooney. Their daughter Cissie Lynn, along with Doug Kershaw, recorded a song titled "The Butcher Holler Moonshine Song: Thunder on the Mountain." Additionally, Belmont Farm Distillery produces Butcher Holler Moonshine as a nod to Loretta's childhood home, which was made famous in her 1969 song "Coal Miner's Daughter" and the 1980 movie of the same name.

A niche genre of moonshine singers was born with performers like Charlie Poole (1892 – 1931)—a moonshiner who used his profits to buy instruments and was part of the North Carolina Ramblers—and Rosa Lee Carson (1909 – 1992)—who was popular in the 1910s and 1920s, and assumed the stage name Moonshine Kate and included moonshine references in many of her songs.

Also, Hank Williams Jr. helped to legally launch the late XXX-icon Popcorn Sutton's moonshine called Popcorn Sutton's Tennessee White Whiskey. He also attended Popcorn's funeral in 2009.

In 1962, the old-time string band New Lost City Ramblers recorded the album *American Moonshine and Prohibition*. This compilation of seventeen tracks is a time capsule treasury of songs reflecting all angles of the moonshine and Prohibition eras. Singles include: "Drunkard's Hiccups," "Bootlegger's Story," "The Moonshiner," "Old Homebrew," "Whiskey Seller," "Prohibition Is a Failure," "The Teetotals," "Wreck on the Highway," "Al Smith for President," and "Down to the Stillhouse to Get a Litter Cider."

In the album's liner notes—which serve as a historical and cultural-snapshot primer on the subject—band member Mike Seeger explains the ongoing partnership between music and liquor, especially as it's depicted on the album. He writes how the songs showcase "reflections on one's own drinking"; the moonshiner's "philosophy and experiences"; the "issue of Prohibition on a realistic level"; and also encompass "anti-drink songs written either by those who would have nothing to do with liquor, who would not even try to understand those who did, or by those who had 'given it up' after initial experiences with it."

With its obvious connotations to moonshine running, bootleg recording refers to a video or song that is unauthorized and released illegally. Pirate radio—unregulated or illegal transmissions—is also known as bootleg radio and the offending stations are known as bootleg stations.

Being the multi-tasking entertainer it is, a glance at song catalogs across genres proves that moonshine as a media star has definite cross-over appeal with starring and cameo roles in songs like Van Morrison's "Moonshine Whiskey" (written by Van Morrison); The Grateful Dead's "Brown-Eyed Women" (written by Jerry Garcia and Robert Hunter, and: incorrectly written

as "Brown-Eyed Woman" on the album's song list); James Taylor's "Copperline" (written by James Taylor and Reynolds Price); George Clinton's Funk-band Parliament's "Moonshine Heather" (written by George Clinton); John Denver's "Take Me Home, Country Roads" (written by John Denver, Taffy Danoff, and William T. Danoff); Beach Boy Dennis Wilson's "Moonshine" (written by Dennis Wilson and Gregg Jakobson); Steve Earle's "Copperhead Road" (written by Steve Earle); Jimmy Buffett's "God's Own Drunk" (written by Lord Buckley); Metallica's "Whiskey in the Jar" (written by Eric Bell, Brian Downey, and Phil Lynott); Aerosmith's "Rag Doll" (written by Steven Tyler, Joe Perry, Jim Vallance, and Holly Knight); and Bruno Mars's "Moonshine" (written by Philip Lawrence, Ari Levine, Andrew Wyatt, Jeffrey Bhasker, Peter Hernandez, and Mark Ronson).

XXX Movie Star

Moonshiners and moonshine were initially immortalized on the Big Screen in 1958's black-and-white *Thunder Road*, starring Robert Mitchum as Lucas Doolin—a moonshine runner in Tennessee and Kentucky. The film embodies the backwoods moonshine lifestyle: hidden stills, family loyalty, Southern grit and charm, relentless revenuers, car chases, and gangsters, along with a little romance thrown in to spice things up even more.

Lucas Doolin's monologue in the movie succinctly pays homage to the history and rebel heart of moonshiners: "You know I remember when I was a little kid, trailing my daddy up to the still through those mountain winters. I suppose I knew then that what he was doing was contrary to somebody's law, but my granddaddy and his daddy before him and so on clear back to Ireland, they held that what a man did on his own land was his business. . . . When they came here, fought for this country, scratched up the hills with their plows and skinny mules, they did it to guarantee the basic rights of free men. They just figured that whiskey makin' was one of 'em."

Fifteen years later, Burt Reynolds introduced moonshine to a new generation when he starred as Gator McKlusky in 1973's *White Lightning* and its 1976 sequel, *Gator*. In *White Lightning*, Reynolds plays a jailed moonshiner who teams up with the authorities to avenge his brother's murder and expose the corrupt sheriff who is responsible for the death and who is also taking bribes from moonshiners. The sequel finds Reynolds as Gator living back with his family in the Okefenokee Swamp and once more taking up the family moonshine business when the law comes looking for his help again.

The role of Lucas Doolin's little brother, Robin, was originally created for Elvis Presley. But because of salary disputes, the role went to Mitchum's real-life son, James, instead.

In 1976, *Moonshine County Express*—the story of three sisters taking over their dad's moonshine business—was released with the tagline: "100 proof women runnin shine cross the county line!"

Reynolds again donned the role of bootlegger when he starred in 1977's *Smokey and the Bandit*. This time, Reynolds was trucker Bo "Bandit" Darville, who is hired to bootleg a load of Coors beer from Texarkana to Atlanta while evading a determined smokey—CB slang for highway patrol officer. During the same year, *Thunder and Lightning*, starring David Carradine and Kate Jackson, followed the adventures of Florida moonshiners.

A cottage industry of films has evolved that are based on real-life moonshiners and bootleggers. These include 1973's *The Last American*

Hero, which was based on the life of legendary bootlegger and NASCAR's first superstar champion, Junior Johnson, who was played by Beau Bridges. And 1975's *Moonrunners*, starring James Mitchum, is based on the life of moonshiner Jerry Rushing, who even appeared briefly in the movie.

Moonrunners, which was narrated by Waylon Jennings as the Balladeer and which revolved around the daring exploits of cousins and bootleggers Grady and Bobby Lee Hagg, was later adapted for television as the hit show *The Dukes of Hazzard* featuring cousins Bo and Luke Duke.

In 1977, *Greased Lightning* starring Richard Pryor was released. The film is loosely based on the life of Wendell Scott, the U.S.'s first African-American stock car racing champion. And 2011's *Red Dirt Rising* follows the life journey of early stock car racer and moonshine hauler Jimmie Lewallen and his friends and family in North Carolina.

More recently, 2012's *Lawless*—starring Shia LaBeouf and Tom Hardy, and based on Matt Bondurant's historical novel about his bootlegging grandfather and great-uncles titled *The Wettest County in the World*—depicted the famed Bondurant brothers of Franklin County, Virginia, as they butted heads with the authorities. *Lawless* further helped the real-life Franklin County cement its place in history as the "Moonshine Capital of the World."

Big 'Shine on the Little Screen

On televisions across the country, starting in black and white and moving into the era of color TV, moonshine debuted its comedic chops and helped several series also become legends for the ages.

Beneath the laughter and the larger-than-life characters, there was a reflection of authentic moonshine culture.

In their own ways, three fictional series in particular captured the essence, the fun, the history, and the heritage of moonshiners and their white lightning: *The Beverly Hillbillies*, *The Waltons*, and *The Dukes of Hazzard*. All three classics are now either available on DVD or in syndication, for full-fledged moonshiner binge-watching marathons.

Moonshine has also had supporting roles and cameos in such films as 1953's *Stalag 17* wherein star William Holden as Sergeant Sefton runs a distillery; and 1969's *True Grit* and 1975's *Rooster Cogburn* in which John Wayne stars as U.S. Marshall Ruben J. "Rooster" Cogburn, who makes no secret of his love for moonshine. In 2009's *Inglourious Basterds,* white lightning gets an A-list plug when Brad Pitt's character Lieutenant Aldo Raine declares, "I done my share of bootleggin'. Up there, if you engage in what the federal government calls illegal activity, but what we call a man just trying to earn a living for his family selling moonshine liquor, it behooves oneself to keep his wits."

Granny's "Spring Tonic" on *The Beverly Hillbillies* (1962 to 1971).

With a bustling homemade still out by the mansion pool in Beverly Hills, Granny's moonshine—that she affectionately called her "spring tonic"—flowed through many of the hit show's episodes. In one particular scene from Season 2, Episode 26, which aired during the 1964 presidential election pitting Democrat incumbent President Lyndon Johnson against Republican Senator Barry Goldwater, Jed and

Granny Clampett discuss how a good dose of her spring tonic is just what's needed to straighten out the Democrats and Republicans in Washington, D.C.

"They need tonic'in, do they?" Jed asks.

Granny minces no words: "The Republicans claim that the Democrats is dragging their feet and the Democrats come back and say that the Republicans ain't got a leg to stand on! . . . That's why I ain't taking no chances. I'm tonic'in both sides!"

This scene is not only a hilarious sign of the times—and many a modern-day moonshiner and citizen might argue it's as relevant today as back then, but it's also a subtle allusion to moonshine as historic rabble-rouser and thorn in the side of politicians and law enforcement.

"Papa's Recipe" doled out by the Baldwin sisters—
Miss Mamie and Miss Emily—on *The Waltons* (1972 to 1981).

Earl Hamner, Jr., whose novel *Spencer's Mountain* inspired the TV series *The Waltons*, created the Baldwin characters and their heirloom moonshine concoction based on a very special memory from growing up in the Blue Ridge Mountains, as noted on The-Waltons.com: "Down on Route 6 between Esmont and Scottsville lived two ladies who made an elixir they referred to as their Papa's Recipe. They were proud of their product, and whenever anyone would sample it, they would lean over, watch them and wait anxiously for a reaction. . . . I wasn't old enough to sample the Recipe but my father and uncles stopped there quite often and they seemed to find the Recipe much to their satisfaction."

And, the Duke family—Uncle Jesse, Bo, Luke, and Daisy—
for whom a rich lineage of moonshine, bootlegging, and
foiling the law ran through their veins on *The Dukes of
Hazzard* (1979 to 1985).

In Episode 3 of Season 1, *The Dukes of Hazzard* Balladeer—narrator Waylon Jennings—summed up the Dukes and all their Southern brethren perfectly during a high-speed bootlegging chase between Bo and Luke and the cops when he said, "Seems like everybody's daddy in Hazzard County used to run moonshine at one time or another."

Just like in the movies, moonshine has made its fair share of cameos on television shows as well. In Season 1, Episode 4 of 1980's *Sanford*, Fred Sanford discovers his pal Cal is whipping up moonshine and begins thinking how he might get in on the action to make some money—and installs a still in the kitchen. Throughout the run of *M*A*S*H* (1972 to 1983), characters Hawkeye Pierce and Trapper John McIntyre operated a homemade distillery in the

Swamp. Meanwhile, Homer Simpson forgoes his thirst quencher of choice, beer, when he befriends a group of moonshiners for whom he becomes a very willing taste tester in 2009's Season 21, Episode 7 of *The Simpsons*.

Moonshine has also popped up on other shows like *Hatfields & McCoys: White Lightning*, *Oz*, *MythBusters*, *The Unit*, *The Real Housewives of Orange County*, and *It's Always Sunny in Philadelphia*.

Lane Cake is also known as Shiny Cake, Prize Cake, and Alabama Lane Cake, and was originally invented by Emma Rylander Lane of Clayton, Alabama. In 2016, it became the official state cake of Alabama—a state that knows its way around a moonshine still. After Emma's cake won first place at a county fair in Georgia, she included it in her 1898 self-published cookbook *A Few Good Things to Eat*. In his memoir *Christmas in Plains*, President Jimmy Carter fondly writes about how his father would welcome holiday guests by baking a few Lanes Cakes.

On the shoulders of these appearances and white lightning's rise from 1700's revolutionary to pop culture stardom, no other program has given the world the behind-the-scenes, close-up look at moonshiners and the moonshine industry like Discovery Channel's docu-series *Moonshiners*. Through multiple top-rated seasons, *Moonshiners* has brought viewers along for the ride into the hollows and dirt-road kingdoms of the industry's most colorful, homespun superstars—folks like Tim, Tickle, and Popcorn; Jim Tom, Patti, and Chico; Digger, Josh, and even a rescue mutt named Cutie Pie.

Moonshiners has invoked the down-home wit and humor that

has made moonshine's artisans the country's most beloved masters of distilling and entertains viewers while celebrating moonshine's spirited thread through our cultural tapestry. As a twenty-first-century historical marker, *Moonshiners* is the ultimate portrait of moonshine as both enduring and original American desperado, and as the new American dream for boozy entrepreneurs. And it proves that moonshine's tap on history is far from over.

Moonshine on the Bookshelf

Moonshine has appeared in several works of literature—both fiction and nonfiction—throughout the twentieth century onward.

In 1960's *To Kill a Mockingbird*, drinking moonshine was one of the reasons Boo Radley, as a rowdy teen, was confined to his house by his dad. "According to neighborhood legend," Harper Lee wrote, "when the younger Radley boy was in his teens he became acquainted with some of the Cunninghams from Old Sarum . . . and they formed the nearest thing to a gang ever seen in Maycomb. They did little, but enough to be discussed by the town and publicly warned from three pulpits: . . . they experimented with stumphole whiskey."

Moonshine has inspired video game creators and gamers. The *Grand Theft Auto* series (*Vice City* and *Vice City Stories*) uses a moonshine-inspired booze called "Boomshine"; for the *Fallout* series, moonshine is used to raise a player's strength; and moonshine is consumed to improve a player's health in *BioShock*. Players of *Redneck Rampage* use moonshine to increase their fighting stamina, while in *Red Dead Redemption*, moonshine is used to refill a player's Dead Eye Meter. And, moonshine induces an out-of-body experience in *Alan Wake*.

And on a much lighter note, XXX appeared under the nickname shinny, which was a title-ingredient when baking Shinny Cake—better known as Lane Cake, which Miss Maudie Atkinson gives to Aunt Alexandria.

While Harper Lee may have been referring to bourbon whiskey, it's fun to let the mind wonder when Scout declares, "Miss Maudie baked a Lane cake so loaded with shinny it made me tight."

Elmore Leonard's 1969 novel *The Moonshine War* transports readers back to Prohibition-era America, pitting a Kentucky moonshiner against corrupt city slickers looking to rob him blind of his corn liquor. *The Moonshine War* was adapted into a movie of the same name in 1970, starring Richard Widmark and Alan Alda.

When it comes to moonshiners, bootleggers, and white lightning on the written page, Matt Bondurant's 2008 fictional history *The Wettest County in the World* is a modern-day classic. "Wettest" being the key word and set in the "Moonshine Capital of the World" Franklin County, Virginia, the novel—which takes place during the 1920s and 1930s—is based on Matt's bootlegging paternal grandfather Jack and his two brothers, Forrest and Howard. The plot is crafted around the real-life event known as the Great Franklin County Moonshine Conspiracy and the ensuing 1935 trial in the foothills of the Blue Ridge Mountains. In 2008, the novel was adapted into a movie titled *Lawless*, starring Shia LaBeouf, Tom Hardy, and Gary Oldman.

A moonshine called Lohocla (alcohol spelled backwards) played an integral role in novelist Patrick Dennis' 1964 fictional biography *First Lady: My Thirty Days Upstairs at the White House, by Martha Dinwiddie Butterfield*.

And Homer "Sonny" Hickman Jr.'s 1998 memoir *Rocket Boys*—later re-titled *October Sky*, describes moonshine being used as an ingredient in the fuel for one of his and his friend's experiments.

Moonshine has also been the subject of scenes and chapters in other memoirs, such as *The Mountains Within Me* by Zell Miller (1975), *A Childhood: The Biography of a Place* by Harry Crews (1978), *The Last Radio Baby* by Raymond Andrews (1990), *Me and My Likker* by Popcorn Sutton (1999), *Ecology of a Cracker Childhood* by Janisse Ray (2000), and *Ava's Man* by Rick Bragg (2002).

The moonshiners' and moonshine's influence across concert stage, screen, and page has further solidified their place in the heart and revelry of America. This burgeoning affection and popularity also laid the groundwork for a modern-day renaissance.

The Moonshiner's Lane Cake

For the Cake:

3 ¼ cups all-purpose flour

1 tablespoon baking powder

¾ teaspoon salt

1 cup butter or margarine, softened

2 cups sugar

2 teaspoons vanilla extract

8 egg whites, divided by twos, or egg replacer

1 cup almond or coconut milk

Preheat the oven to 375° F.

In a medium bowl, sift the flour, baking powder, and salt together. In another medium bowl, cream the butter and then add the sugar and vanilla, stirring to combine. Adding 2 egg whites at a time, add all 8 egg whites, mixing well. Using a wooden spoon, fold in the flour mixture alternately with the almond milk, beginning and ending with the flour.

Line 4 ungreased 9-inch cake pans with waxed paper. Divide the cake batter evenly among the pans. Bake the cake layers at 375° F for 20 minutes or until a toothpick inserted in the center comes out clean. Remove the pans from the oven and cool for a few minutes.

For the Filling:

8 egg yolks or egg replacer
1 cup sugar
½ cup butter or margarine, softened
½ to 1 cup each (to equal 3 to 4 cups total)
your choice of:
    raisins, pecans (chopped), coconut, cherries
    (chopped), or dates (chopped)
½ cup unflavored moonshine or infused moonshine,
to taste
1 teaspoon vanilla extract, or to taste

In a large saucepan, using a mixer or wooden spoon, beat the egg yolks. Next, using a wooden spoon, fold in the sugar followed by the butter. Over a medium to high heat, cook the mixture until it is thick, stirring, about 5 to 7 minutes. Remove the saucepan from the heat. Stir in the fruit and nuts, moonshine, and vanilla. Allow the mixture to cool.

To Assemble the Cake:

Using a spatula, spread the filling evenly between the 4 cake layers. Ice the entire cake with your homemade or store-bought frosting of choice. Garnish as desired with cherries or other slices of fruit.

Yields 1 Moonshiner's Lane Cake, approximately 8 to 10 servings.

Moonshiners Hall of Fame

Mrs. Willie Carter Sharpe

One of the great moonshine runners of all time, Willie Carter Sharpe is said to have hauled over more than a hundred thousand gallons of hooch during the late 1920s and early 1930s in and around Franklin County, Virginia. She is known as the "Queen of Roanoke Rumrunners."

CHAPTER 9

The New Golden Age of Moonshiners

A ll-American.

   Immigrant. Artisan. Adventurer. Revolutionary. Rebel. Outlaw. Daredevil. Patriot. Entrepreneur. Change maker. Reveler. Tourist draw. Superstar. Icon. Living history.

Moonshiners and their moonshine have endured the forces of nature and humankind, and have remained remarkably unchanged for more than two hundred years and across the threshold of a new millennium.

Now, the next role for moonshiners is that of Renaissance men and women. The children, grandchildren, and even great-grandchildren of moonshine pioneers are now taking family tradition and heirloom recipes into the new American frontier of the twenty-first century. Craftsmen, creatives, and entrepreneurs themselves, they're preserving cultural roots, while adding contemporary twists and branches of their own to the collective moonshine tree.

Today, it is legal to own a still, but only for decorative purposes. However, a permit called a Federal Distilled Spirits Permit is required to distill alcohol for personal or commercial use. Also, states vary in their distillation laws.

Moonshine rolls with the punches and the times. And its time is always *right now*.

To begin with: Moonshine now has its own holiday. The first Thursday in June is National Moonshine Day.

Museums—like the Franklin County History Museum and Research Center in Rocky Mount, Virginia; Wilkes Heritage Museum in Wilkesboro, North Carolina; Baker Block Museum in Baker, Florida; The Foxfire Museum & Heritage Center in Clayton, Georgia; The Museum of the American Cocktail in New Orleans, Louisiana; Museum of Ashe County History in Jefferson, North Carolina; and local and state historical associations—now curate moonshine-inspired artifacts, personal histories, and exhibitions. The Franklin County Historical Society in Virginia even hosts an annual Moonshine Express tour that features costumed actors and historical moonshiner sites in the area.

> "Jesus turned water into wine. I turned it into liquor."
>
> ~ Popcorn Sutton

The NASCAR Hall of Fame in Charlotte, North Carolina, also has a collection of moonshine-related memorabilia alluding to XXX's role during the early days of racing. A popular exhibit is the moonshine still created by Junior Johnson especially for the NASCAR Hall of Fame when it opened in 2010.

In 2004, the Distilled Spirits Council launched the American Whiskey Trail tourism initiative to celebrate the cultural heritage and history of spirits, such as moonshine, in America. The American Whiskey Trail includes museums, such as the Allegheny Museum in Cumberland, Maryland; Oscar Getz Museum of Whiskey History in Bardstown, Kentucky; and Whiskey Rebellion sites such as Oliver Miller Homestead in South Park, Pennsylvania, and Woodville Plantation, the John and Presley Neville House in Bridgeville, Pennsylvania.

Distilleries are also part of the American Whiskey Trail. These include icons like Jack Daniel's in Lynchburg, Tennessee; Jim Beam in Clermont, Kentucky; Maker's Mark in Loretto, Kentucky; and

Wild Turkey in Lawrenceburg, Tennessee. Also included are George Washington's Distillery at Historic Mount Vernon in Alexandria, Virginia; George Dickel in Tullahoma, Tennessee; Stitzel-Weller Distillery in Louisville, Kentucky; and Woodford Reserve in Versailles, Kentucky.

Southern Grace Distilleries in Mt. Pleasant, North Carolina, holds the distinction of being the only distillery in the U.S. housed in a former prison where folks were sentenced to a year and one day for moonshining. Operating as a prison from 1929 to 2011, moonshiners were held there into the 1970s. For current president and CEO, Leanne Powell, whose grandfather was a bootlegger, running Southern Grace Distilleries is about proudly carrying on a family tradition, *legally*.

Moonshine festivals have been popular for years and have done their part to preserve the history of moonshiners and their XXX. These include the Virginia Moonshine Festival in Richmond, Virginia; the New Straitsville Moonshine Festival in New Straitsville, Ohio; the Mountain Moonshine Festival in Dawsonville, Georgia; and the Franklin County Moonshine Fest in Rocky Mount, Virginia. Also, the Allegheny Museum and Historic Downtown Washington, Pennsylvania, both host Whiskey Rebellion Festivals.

The hub of today's moonshine industry is no longer concentrated along woodland creeks, hollers, and farms, but rather in the legal distilleries that most often have been built on the foundation of an old family recipe or local links to moonshine heritage.

One of the most famous is Ole Smokey Tennessee Moonshine in Gatlinburg, Tennessee. Opened in 2010, it was the first federally licensed distillery—nicknamed the Holler—in Tennessee. Co-founder and criminal lawyer Joe Baker has deep roots in the area and its moonshine ancestry, which includes a family recipe that's over two hundred years old. Ole Smokey has become the country's most visited distillery. It is a blueprint for moonshining in the twenty-first century, including a world-famous Apple Pie Moonshine, targeted marketing, tours, a tasting room, and a daily bluegrass band and rocking chairs for visitors.

Piedmont Distillers, Inc. is also leaving its mark on the industry. Founded in 2005, Piedmont Distillers is North Carolina's first legal distillery since Prohibition. It is also home base for Junior Johnson's popular Midnight Moon line of moonshine, as well as the Catdaddy brand.

The "Moonshine Capital of the World," Franklin County, Tennessee, now has two legal distilleries: Franklin County Distilleries in Boones Hill and Twin Creeks Distillery in Rocky Mount. Franklin County Distilleries, started by physician Dan Hodges, is the first legal, post-Prohibition distillery in Franklin County. Meanwhile, Twin Creeks Distillery founder Chris Prillaman charts his family's moonshine history back to two great-grandfathers, one of whom was involved in the 1935 Franklin Moonshine Conspiracy scandal.

Moonshine has even united the country's most famous feuding families, who created Hatfield & McCoy Moonshine. Handcrafted in small batches in Gilbert, West Virginia, the heirloom recipe—bearing the tagline "Drink of the Devil"—was created by patriarch Devil Anse Hatfield in the 1800s and handed down through the generations.

The first legal moonshine distillery in South Carolina was Palmetto Distillery, founded by brothers Trey and Bryan Boggs in Anderson in 2011. The Boggs moonshine tradition goes back to folk musician and moonshine/bootlegger Dock Boggs in the early 1900s.

Gatlinburg's Sugarlands Distilling Company in the Sugarlands area of the Great Smokey Mountains known as Moonshiners' Paradise has merged past and present with its Legends Series brand of moonshine. The various Legends recipes are by stars of Discovery Channel's *Moonshiners*—Mark Rogers, Digger Manes, Mark Ramsey, Jim Tom Hedrick, and Steven Ray Tickle. Among them, these moonshiners have nearly two hundred years of experience.

Moonshiners star Tim Smith has also bridged past with present, by going legit with his Climax Moonshine. Using Tim's original recipe, the moonshine is produced using corn, rye, and barley malt at Belmont Farm Distillery in Culpepper, Virginia. Every bottle of Climax Moonshine bears the image of Tim's dog, Camo, who has become one of the biggest four-legged stars in the industry.

The new Golden Age of Moonshiners is in full swing, and shows no signs of slowing down. Moonshiners have now achieved the validation and victory they've sought from the beginning. And drinkers get to reap the ultimate benefit by enjoying moonshine whenever and wherever they want. Liquor stores have entire sections dedicated to moonshine, while bars and restaurants across the United States lure customers with pure white lightning and artisanal moonshine cocktails.

New England's first legal moonshine since Prohibition is Onyx Moonshine, which debuted in 2011. It's produced in East Hartford, Connecticut.

From the hollers of Appalachia to bustling city avenues, it's celebration time. Four hundred years after George Thorpe distilled the first corn whiskey in the Thirteen Colonies—through the toils of revolution, hiding, running, temperance, protest, revenuers, Prohibition, and government crackdowns—moonshiners finally got the last laugh.

Moonshiner Mark Ramsey, who once built stills for Popcorn Sutton and Digger Manes, was trained in the moonshine craft by Popcorn.

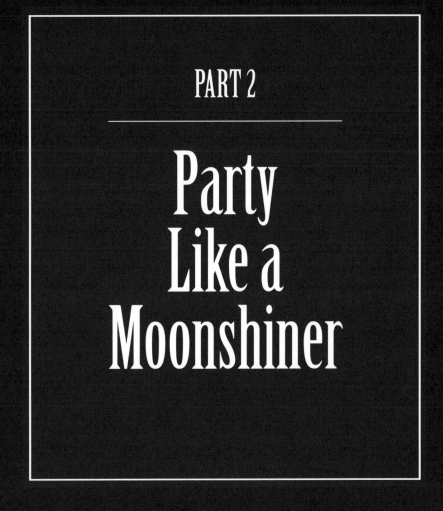

PART 2

Party
Like a
Moonshiner

CHAPTER 10

Moonshine Infusions

Crafting moonshine infusions at home is not only easy, but it's your chance to play moonshiner without having to perfect the 180-getaway maneuver or hide your operations along a creek in Appalachia.

The following pages offer more than fifty fruit, vegetable, berry, herb and spice, candy, and even wildflower infusions that take only a few minutes to prepare and can often be stored in the freezer for up to a month or more. While the directions for infusing moonshine are similar across the board, sometimes certain infusions need to sit a little longer than others for maximum flavor, as noted in the recipes that follow.

The finished infusions can then be enjoyed as sippers on the rocks—either solo or as part of a fun moonshine sampling with friends—or used as inspired ingredients that will transform any cocktail into an artisanal masterpiece to be savored. Many of the following infusions are used in the moonshine cocktail recipes in chapter 11.

Fruit and Berry Moonshine Infusions

Pineapple-Infused Moonshine

- 3 to 4 large slices of fresh pineapple, cut into small cubes (if muddling) or large cubes

- 3 cups unflavored moonshine

Using a 1-quart jar, add the pineapple and lightly muddle if using small cubes or leave larger cubes as is. Pour in the moonshine. Seal the jar with a lid. Shake the mixture. Let sit for 3 days to 1 week, shaking once or twice a day. If using small, muddled pineapple cubes, using a sieve or coffee filter, strain the pineapple-infused moonshine into a new 1-quart jar. Or, if using larger pineapple cubes, serve from the original jar and garnish servings with the moonshine-infused pineapple cubes. Serve immediately or cover and store in freezer for up to 1 month.

Yields approximately 3 cups.

Peach-Infused Moonshine

- 4 to 5 large fresh peaches, peeled and cut into small cubes (if muddling) or wedges

- 3 cups unflavored moonshine

Using a 1-quart jar, add the peaches and lightly muddle if using small cubes or leave the wedges as is. Pour in the moonshine. Seal the jar with a lid. Shake the mixture. Let sit for 3 days to 1 week, shaking once or twice a day. If using small, muddled peach cubes, using a sieve or coffee filter, strain the peach-infused moonshine into a new 1-quart jar. Or, if using peach wedges, serve from the original jar and garnish servings with the moonshine-infused peach wedges. Serve immediately or cover and store in freezer for up to 1 month.

Yields approximately 3 cups.

Grapefruit-Infused Moonshine

- 3 to 4 large slices of fresh grapefruit, cut into small cubes (if muddling) or large cubes

- 3 cups unflavored moonshine

Using a 1-quart jar, add the grapefruit and lightly muddle if using small cubes or leave larger cubes as is. Pour in the moonshine. Seal the jar with a lid. Shake the mixture. Let sit for 3 days to 1 week, shaking once or twice a day. If using small, muddled grapefruit cubes, using a sieve or coffee filter, strain the grapefruit-infused moonshine into a new 1-quart jar. Or, if using larger grapefruit cubes, serve from the original jar and garnish servings with the moonshine-infused grapefruit cubes. Serve immediately or cover and store in freezer for up to 1 month.

Yields approximately 3 cups.

Orange-Infused Moonshine

- 1 to 2 large fresh oranges, peeled and cut into small cubes (if muddling) or wedges

- 3 cups unflavored moonshine

Using a 1-quart jar, add the oranges and lightly muddle if using small cubes or leave the wedges as is. Pour in the moonshine. Seal the jar with a lid. Shake the mixture. Let sit for 3 days to 1 week, shaking once or twice a day. If using small, muddled orange cubes, using a sieve or coffee filter, strain the orange-infused moonshine into a new 1-quart jar. Or, if using orange wedges, serve from the original jar and garnish servings with the moonshine-infused orange wedges. Serve immediately or cover and store in freezer for up to 1 month.

Yields approximately 3 cups.

Watermelon-Infused Moonshine

- 5 to 6 large slices of fresh watermelon, cut into small cubes

- 3 cups unflavored moonshine

Using a 1-quart jar, add the watermelon and lightly muddle. Pour in the moonshine. Seal the jar with a lid. Shake the mixture. Let sit for 1 week, shaking once or twice a day. Using a sieve or coffee filter, strain the watermelon-infused moonshine into a new 1-quart jar. Serve immediately or cover and store in freezer for up to 1 month.

Yields approximately 3 cups.

Lemon Lime-
Infused Moonshine

- 2 small fresh lemons, peeled and cut into wedges (or omit for just Lime-Infused Moonshine)

- 2 small fresh limes, peeled and cut into wedges (or omit for just Lemon-Infused Moonshine)

- 3 cups unflavored moonshine

Using a 1-quart jar, add the lemon and lime wedges and lightly muddle. Pour in the moonshine. Seal the jar with a lid. Shake the mixture. Let sit for 3 days to 1 week, shaking once or twice a day. Using a sieve or coffee filter, strain the lemon lime–infused moonshine into a new 1-quart jar. Serve immediately or cover and store in freezer for up to 1 month.

Yields approximately 3 cups.

Pear-Infused Moonshine

- 4 to 5 large fresh pears, peeled and cut into small cubes (if muddling) or wedges

- 3 cups unflavored moonshine

Using a 1-quart jar, add the pears and lightly muddle if using small cubes or leave the wedges as is. Pour in the moonshine. Seal the jar with a lid. Shake the mixture. Let sit for 3 days to 1 week, shaking once or twice a day. If using small, muddled pear cubes, using a sieve or coffee filter, strain the pear-infused moonshine into a new 1-quart jar. Or, if using pear wedges, serve from the original jar and garnish servings with the moonshine-infused pear wedges. Serve immediately or cover and store in freezer for up to 1 month.

Yields approximately 3 cups.

Cherry-Infused Moonshine

- 1 ½ cups fresh cherries, washed, stemmed, and pitted, whole or halved, or maraschino cherries

- 3 cups unflavored moonshine

Using a 1-quart jar, add the cherries. Pour in the moonshine. Seal the jar with a lid. Let sit for 2 to 3 weeks, shaking once or twice a day. Shake the mixture. Either serve directly from the jar, leaving the cherries as is; or, using a sieve or coffee filter, strain the cherry-infused moonshine into a new 1-quart jar, and save the moonshine-infused cherries for garnishing. Serve immediately or cover and store in freezer for up to 1 month.

Yields approximately 3 cups.

Apple-Infused Moonshine

- 2 large fresh apples, peeled and cut into small cubes (if muddling) or wedges

- 3 cups unflavored moonshine

Using a 1-quart jar, add the apples and lightly muddle if using small cubes or leave the wedges as is. Pour in the moonshine. Seal the jar with a lid. Shake the mixture. Let sit for 3 days to 1 week, shaking once or twice a day. If using small, muddled apple cubes, using a sieve or coffee filter, strain the apple-infused moonshine into a new 1-quart jar. Or, if using apple wedges, serve from the original jar and garnish servings with the moonshine-infused apple wedges. Serve immediately or cover and store in freezer for up to 1 month.

Yields approximately 3 cups.

Plum-Infused Moonshine

- 2 large fresh plums, peeled and quartered

- 3 cups unflavored moonshine

Using a 1-quart jar, add the plums and lightly muddle. Pour in the moonshine. Seal the jar with a lid. Shake the mixture. Let sit for 3 to 5 days, shaking once or twice a day. Using a sieve or coffee filter, strain the plum-infused moonshine into a new 1-quart jar. Serve immediately or cover and store in freezer for up to 1 month.

Yields approximately 3 cups.

Apricot-Infused Moonshine

- 4 large fresh apricots, chopped

- 3 cups unflavored moonshine

Using a 1-quart jar, add the apricots and lightly muddle. Pour in the moonshine. Seal the jar with a lid. Shake the mixture. Let sit for 5 days to 1 week, shaking once or twice a day. Using a sieve or coffee filter, strain the apricot-infused moonshine into a new 1-quart jar. Serve immediately or cover and store in freezer for up to 1 month.

Yields approximately 3 cups.

Kiwi-Infused Moonshine

- 4 large fresh kiwis, peeled and sliced

- 3 cups unflavored moonshine

Using a 1-quart jar, add the kiwis and lightly muddle. Pour in the moonshine. Seal the jar with a lid. Shake the mixture. Let sit for 1 week, shaking once or twice a day. Using a sieve or coffee filter, strain the kiwi-infused moonshine into a new 1-quart jar. Serve immediately or cover and store in freezer for up to 1 month.

Yields approximately 3 cups.

Mango-Infused Moonshine

- 3 to 4 large slices of fresh mango,
  cut into small cubes (if muddling)
  or large cubes

- 3 cups unflavored moonshine

Using a 1-quart jar, add the mango and lightly muddle
if using small cubes or leave larger cubes as is. Pour in the
moonshine. Seal the jar with a lid. Shake the mixture. Let sit for
3 days to 1 week, shaking once or twice a day. If using small,
muddled mango cubes, using a sieve or coffee filter, strain the
mango-infused moonshine into a new 1-quart jar. Or, if using
larger mango cubes, serve from the original jar and garnish
servings with the moonshine-infused mango cubes. Serve
immediately or cover and store in freezer for up to 1 month.

Yields approximately 3 cups.

Banana-Infused Moonshine

- 2 large fresh bananas, cut into chunks

- 3 cups unflavored moonshine

Using a 1-quart jar, add the banana and lightly muddle. Pour in the moonshine. Seal the jar with a lid. Shake the mixture. Let sit for 1 to 3 days, shaking once or twice a day. Using a sieve or coffee filter, strain the banana-infused moonshine into a new 1-quart jar. Serve immediately or cover and store in freezer for up to 1 month.

Yields approximately 3 cups.

Coconut-Infused Moonshine

- 2 ½ cups coconut flakes

- 3 cups unflavored moonshine

Using a 1-quart jar, add the coconut. Pour in the moonshine. Seal the jar with a lid. Shake the mixture. Let sit for 1 to 2 weeks, shaking once or twice a day. Using a sieve or coffee filter, strain the coconut-infused moonshine into a new 1-quart jar. Serve immediately or cover and store in freezer for up to 1 month.

Yields approximately 3 cups.

Olive-Infused Moonshine

- 2 ½ cups green olives

- 3 cups unflavored moonshine

Using a 1-quart jar, add the olives and lightly muddle. Pour in the moonshine. Seal the jar with a lid. Shake the mixture. Let sit for 3 days to 1 week, shaking once or twice a day. Using a sieve or coffee filter, strain the olive-infused moonshine into a new 1-quart jar. Serve immediately or cover and store in freezer for up to 1 month.

Yields approximately 3 cups.

Nutty-Infused Moonshine

- 2 cups crushed nuts of choice, individual or mixture, such as hazelnut, almond, pecan, peanut, Brazil nut, macadamia, or cashews

- 3 cups unflavored moonshine

Using a 1-quart jar, add the nuts. Pour in the moonshine. Seal the jar with a lid. Shake the mixture. Let sit for 1 to 2 weeks, shaking once or twice a day. Using a sieve or coffee filter, strain the nut-infused moonshine into a new 1-quart jar. Serve immediately or cover and store in freezer for up to 1 month.

Yields approximately 3 cups.

Blueberry-Infused Moonshine

- 2 cups fresh blueberries

- 3 cups unflavored moonshine

Using a 1-quart jar, add the blueberries and gently muddle them. Pour in the moonshine. Seal the jar with a lid. Let sit for 1 week, shaking once or twice a day. Shake the mixture. Using a sieve or coffee filter, strain the blueberry-infused moonshine into a new 1-quart jar. Serve immediately or cover and store in freezer for up to 1 month.

Yields approximately 3 cups.

Strawberry-Infused Moonshine

- 1 cup fresh strawberries (left whole or cut into slices or cubes)
- 3 cups unflavored moonshine

Using a 1-quart jar, add the strawberries and gently muddle them (unless left whole). Pour in the moonshine. Seal the jar with a lid. Shake the mixture. Let sit for 1 week, shaking once or twice a day. If using sliced or cubed strawberries, using a sieve or coffee filter, strain the strawberry-infused moonshine into a new 1-quart jar. Or, if leaving the strawberries whole, serve from the original jar and garnish servings with the moonshine-infused strawberries. Serve immediately or cover and store in freezer for up to 1 month.

Yields approximately 3 cups.

Blackberry-Infused Moonshine

- 2 cups fresh blackberries

- 3 cups unflavored moonshine

Using a 1-quart jar, add the blackberries and gently muddle them. Pour in the moonshine. Seal the jar with a lid. Let sit for 1 week, shaking once or twice a day. Shake the mixture. Using a sieve or coffee filter, strain the blackberry-infused moonshine into a new 1-quart jar. Serve immediately or cover and store in freezer for up to 1 month.

Yields approximately 3 cups.

Raspberry-Infused Moonshine

- 2 cups fresh raspberries

- 3 cups unflavored moonshine

Using a 1-quart jar, add the raspberries and gently muddle them. Pour in the moonshine. Seal the jar with a lid. Shake the mixture. Let sit for 1 week, shaking once or twice a day. Using a sieve or coffee filter, strain the raspberry-infused moonshine into a new 1-quart jar. Serve immediately or cover and store in freezer for up to 1 month.

Yields approximately 3 cups.

Cranberry-Infused Moonshine

- 1 pound cranberries, chopped

- 3 cups unflavored moonshine

Using a 1-quart jar, add the cranberries. Pour in the moonshine. Seal the jar with a lid. Shake the mixture. Let sit for 1 to 2 weeks, shaking once or twice a day. Using a sieve or coffee filter, strain the cranberry-infused moonshine into a new 1-quart jar. Serve immediately or cover and store in freezer for up to 1 month.

Yields approximately 3 cups.

Juniper-Infused Moonshine

- 10 to 12 juniper berries, crushed

- 3 cups unflavored moonshine

Using a 1-quart jar, add the juniper berries. Pour in the moonshine. Seal the jar with a lid. Shake the mixture. Let sit for 3 days to 1 week, shaking once or twice a day. Using a sieve or coffee filter, strain the juniper-infused moonshine into a new 1-quart jar. Serve immediately or cover and store in freezer for up to 1 month.

Yields approximately 3 cups.

The Moonshiner's Book Club

Books and booze have become the hallmark of book clubs and reading groups everywhere. For your next book club selection and meeting, make it moonshine themed with these famous moonshine novels and cocktails, along with a few scrumptious slices of the Moonshiner's Lane Cake on page 96.

The Moonshine War by Elmore Leonard

This classic 1969 novel transports readers back to Prohibition-era America, pitting a Kentucky moonshiner against corrupt city slickers looking to rob him blind of his corn liquor. *The Moonshine War* was adapted into a movie of the same name in 1970.

Suggested moonshine cocktails

Mountain Julep (p. 187)

Dirt Road Colada (p. 195)

Shinny Mary (p. 201)

Yell-O Moon Shots (p. 226)

Spiked Georgia Peach (p. 241)

Moonshiner's Strawberry-Orange Slushy (p. 186)

The Wettest County in the World
by Matt Bondurant

This 2008 historical novel is a modern-day classic. Set in the "Moonshine Capital of the World," Franklin County, Virginia, the story—which takes place during the 1920s and 1930s—is based on Matt's bootlegging paternal grandfather Jack and his two brothers, Forrest and Howard. The plot is crafted around the real-life event known as the Great Franklin County Moonshine Conspiracy and the ensuing 1935 trial in the foothills of the Blue Ridge Mountains. In 2008, the book was adapted into a movie titled *Lawless*, starring Shia LaBeouf, Tom Hardy, and Gary Oldman.

Suggested moonshine cocktails
Happy Sally's Sweet Tea (p. 184)
The Bootlegger's Navel (p. 185)
Moonshine Rita (p. 231)
Lemongrass and Mint Mojito (p. 213)
Virginia Pear Mimosa (p. 205)
Appalachian Watermelon Martini (p. 189)

Vegetable and Moonshine Infusions

Cucumber-Infused Moonshine

- 1 large fresh cucumber, cut into small cubes

- 3 cups unflavored moonshine

Using a 1-quart jar, add the cucumber cubes. Pour in the moonshine. Seal the jar with a lid. Shake the mixture. Let sit for 1 week, shaking once or twice a day. Using a sieve or coffee filter, strain the cucumber-infused moonshine into a new 1-quart jar. Serve immediately or cover and store in freezer for up to 1 month.

Yields approximately 3 cups.

Jalapeño-Infused Moonshine

- 2 to 3 jalapeños, stemmed and chopped

- 3 cups unflavored moonshine

Using a 1-quart jar, add the jalapeños. Pour in the moonshine. Seal the jar with a lid. Shake the mixture. Let sit for 2 days to 1 week, shaking once or twice a day. Using a sieve or coffee filter, strain the jalapeño-infused moonshine into a new 1-quart jar. Serve immediately or cover and store in freezer for up to 1 month.

Yields approximately 3 cups.

Peppered Celery-
Infused Moonshine

- 2 cups chopped celery

- 3 tablespoons black pepper

- 3 cups unflavored moonshine

Using a 1-quart jar, add the celery and pepper. Pour in the moonshine. Seal the jar with a lid. Shake the mixture. Let sit for 3 days to 1 week, shaking once or twice a day. Using a sieve or coffee filter, strain the peppered celery–infused moonshine into a new 1-quart jar. Serve immediately or cover and store in freezer for up to 1 month.

Yields approximately 3 cups.

Garlic-Infused Moonshine

- 1 large bulb garlic, separated into cloves and peeled

- 3 cups unflavored moonshine

Using a 1-quart jar, add the garlic. Pour in the moonshine. Seal the jar with a lid. Shake the mixture. Let sit for 3 days, shaking once or twice a day. Using a sieve or coffee filter, strain the garlic-infused moonshine into a new 1-quart jar. Serve immediately or cover and store in freezer for up to 1 month.

Yields approximately 3 cups.

Carrot-Infused Moonshine

- 7 large carrots,
  peeled and either cut
  into ribbons or coins

- 3 cups unflavored moonshine

Using a 1-quart jar, add the carrots. Pour in the moonshine. Seal the jar with a lid. Shake the mixture. Let sit for 2 to 3 weeks, shaking once or twice a day. Using a sieve or coffee filter, strain the carrot-infused moonshine into a new 1-quart jar. Serve immediately or cover and store in freezer for up to 1 month.

Yields approximately 3 cups.

Horseradish-Infused Moonshine

- 2 (3-inch) pieces fresh horseradish, peeled and sliced

- 3 cups unflavored moonshine

Using a 1-quart jar, add the horseradish. Pour in the moonshine. Seal the jar with a lid. Shake the mixture. Let sit for 1 week, shaking once or twice a day. Using a sieve or coffee filter, strain the horseradish-infused moonshine into a new 1-quart jar. Serve immediately or cover and store in freezer for up to 1 month.

Yields approximately 3 cups.

Tomato-
Infused Moonshine

- 2 large tomatoes,
  cut into chunks or wedges

- 3 cups unflavored moonshine

Using a 1-quart jar, add the tomatoes. Pour in the moonshine. Seal the jar with a lid. Shake the mixture. Let sit for 1 day, shaking once or twice a day. Using a sieve or coffee filter, strain the tomato-infused moonshine into a new 1-quart jar. Serve the moonshine immediately or cover and store in freezer for up to 1 month.

Yields approximately 3 cups.

Dill Pickle-Infused Moonshine

- 4 to 6 large dill pickle spears, whole or cut into 1-inch pieces

- 3 cups unflavored moonshine

Using a 1-quart jar, add the dill pickles. Pour in the moonshine. Seal the jar with a lid. Shake the mixture. Let sit for 3 days to 1 week, shaking once or twice a day. Using a sieve or coffee filter, strain the dill pickle–infused moonshine into a new 1-quart jar. Serve the moonshine immediately or cover and store in freezer for up to 1 month.

Yields approximately 3 cups.

Beet-Infused Moonshine

- 2 ½ pounds of beets, peeled and cubed

- 3 cups unflavored moonshine

Using a 1-quart jar, add the beets. Pour in the moonshine. Seal the jar with a lid. Shake the mixture. Let sit for 5 days to 1 week, shaking once or twice a day. Using a sieve or coffee filter, strain the beet-infused moonshine into a new 1-quart jar. Serve immediately or cover and store in freezer for up to 1 month.

Yields approximately 3 cups.

Leek-Infused Moonshine

- 2 large leeks, cut into coins

- 3 cups unflavored moonshine

Using a 1-quart jar, add the leeks. Pour in the moonshine. Seal the jar with a lid. Shake the mixture. Let sit for 1 week, shaking once or twice a day. Using a sieve or coffee filter, strain the leek-infused moonshine into a new 1-quart jar. Serve immediately or cover and store in freezer for up to 1 month.

Yields approximately 3 cups.

The Moonshiner's Movie Night

Over the years, numerous movies have been made, starring moonshine and bootleggers. For your next movie night, pop in a moonshine classic and whip up a few moonshine cocktails, and let the show begin.

Thunder Road
Starring Robert Mitchum

This 1958 black-and-white classic focuses on moonshine runner Lucas Doolin (Robert Mitchum) who's working the moonshine circuit across Tennessee and Kentucky. The film embodies the backwoods moonshine lifestyle: hidden stills, family loyalty, Southern grit and charm, relentless revenuers, car chases, and gangsters, along with a little romance thrown in to spice things up even more.

Suggested moonshine cocktails

Moonshine Monkey (p. 183)

Creek Breeze (p. 225)

Howl at the Moon (p. 223)

White Lightning and *Gator*
Starring Burt Reynolds

Make it a double-feature night with 1973's *White Lightning* and its 1976 sequel, *Gator.*

In *White Lightning,* Gator McKlusky (Burt Reynolds) is a jailed moonshiner who teams up with the authorities to avenge his brother's murder and expose the corrupt sheriff who is responsible for the death and who is also taking bribes from moonshiners.

Gator finds Gator McKlusky living back with his family in the Okefenokee Swamp and once more taking up the family moonshine business when the law comes looking for his help again.

Suggested moonshine cocktails
Hillbilly Berry Bush (p. 208)
Smokey Mountain S'more (p. 207)
Old Horsey (p. 248)

The Moonshiner's Movie Night

Smokey and the Bandit

Starring Burt Reynolds and Sally Field

In 1977's *Smokey and the Bandit,* trucker Bo "Bandit" Darville (Burt Reynolds) is hired to bootleg a load of beer from Texarkana to Atlanta while evading a determined Smokey— CB slang for highway patrol officer. While technically not a moonshine movie, bootleggers of any kind are still part of the rebel spirit of moonshine. Plus, it's the perfect excuse to try some of the moonshine and beer cocktails in chapter 11.

Suggested moonshine cocktails

The 180 (p. 222)

Redneck Knockout (p. 214)

Party in the Holler (p. 198)

Lawless
Starring Shia LaBeouf and Tom Hardy

This 2008 film is based on Matt Bondurant's historical novel about his bootlegging grandfather and great-uncles titled *The Wettest County in the World*. It tells the story of the famed Bondurant brothers of Franklin County, Virginia, as they bucked heads with the authorities. Lawless also further helped the real-life Franklin County cement its place in history as the "Moonshine Capital of the World."

Suggested moonshine cocktails

Moonshine Mule (p. 204)

Banana Split (p. 227)

Yell-O Moon Shots (p. 226)

Herb, Spice, and Wildflower
Moonshine Infusions

Basil-Infused Moonshine

- 1 large bunch fresh basil, washed and dried

- 3 cups unflavored moonshine

Using a 1-quart jar, add the basil. Pour in the moonshine. Seal the jar with a lid. Shake the mixture. Let sit for 3 days to 1 week, shaking once or twice a day. Using a sieve or coffee filter, strain the basil-infused moonshine into a new 1-quart jar. Serve immediately or cover and store in freezer for up to 1 month.

Yields approximately 3 cups.

Lemongrass-Infused Moonshine

- 2 cups lemongrass stalks, sliced

- 3 cups unflavored moonshine

Using a 1-quart jar, add the lemongrass and gently muddle. Pour in the moonshine. Seal the jar with a lid. Shake the mixture. Let sit for 1 to 2 weeks, shaking once or twice a day. Using a sieve or coffee filter, strain the lemongrass-infused moonshine into a new 1-quart jar. Serve immediately or cover and store in freezer for up to 1 month.

Yields approximately 3 cups.

Caraway-Infused Moonshine

- 3 tablespoons caraway seeds

- 3 cups unflavored moonshine

Using a 1-quart jar, add the caraway seeds. Pour in the moonshine. Seal the jar with a lid. Shake the mixture. Let sit for 1 to 2 weeks, shaking once or twice a day. Using a sieve or coffee filter, strain the caraway-infused moonshine into a new 1-quart jar. Serve immediately or cover and store in freezer for up to 1 month.

Yields approximately 3 cups.

Anise-Infused Moonshine

- 3 whole star anise and
  2 tablespoons anise seeds

- 3 cups unflavored moonshine

Using a 1-quart jar, add the anise. Pour in the moonshine. Seal the jar with a lid. Let sit for 1 to 2 weeks, shaking once or twice a day. Shake the mixture. Using a sieve or coffee filter, strain the anise-infused moonshine into a new 1-quart jar. Serve immediately or cover and store in freezer for up to 1 month.

Yields approximately 3 cups.

Rosemary-Infused Moonshine

- 2 to 3 sprigs of rosemary

- 3 cups unflavored moonshine

Using a 1-quart jar, add the rosemary. Pour in the moonshine. Seal the jar with a lid. Shake the mixture. Let sit for 3 days to 1 week, shaking once or twice a day. Using a sieve or coffee filter, strain the rosemary-infused moonshine into a new 1-quart jar. Serve immediately or cover and store in freezer for up to 1 month.

Yields approximately 3 cups.

Mint-Infused Moonshine

- 1 ½ cups fresh mint leaves

- 3 cups unflavored moonshine

Using a 1-quart jar, add the mint leaves. Pour in the moonshine. Seal the jar with a lid. Shake the mixture. Let sit for 1 week, shaking once or twice a day. Using a sieve or coffee filter, strain the mint-infused moonshine into a new 1-quart jar. Serve immediately or cover and store in freezer for up to 1 month.

Yields approximately 3 cups.

Old Bay®-
Infused Moonshine

- 1 cup Old Bay® Seasoning

- 3 cups unflavored moonshine

Using a 1-quart jar, add the Old Bay. Pour in the moonshine. Seal the jar with a lid. Shake the mixture. Let sit for 3 days to 1 week, shaking once or twice a day. Using a sieve or coffee filter, strain the Old Bay–infused moonshine into a new 1-quart jar. Serve immediately or cover and store in freezer for up to 1 month.

Yields approximately 3 cups.

Cinnamon-Infused Moonshine

- 4 cinnamon sticks

- 3 cups unflavored moonshine

Using a 1-quart jar, place the cinnamon sticks on the bottom. Pour in the moonshine. Seal the jar with a lid. Shake the mixture. Let sit for 1 week, shaking once or twice a day. Using a sieve or coffee filter, strain the cinnamon-infused moonshine into a new 1-quart jar. Serve immediately or cover and store in freezer for up to 4 months.

Yields approximately 3 cups.

Ginger-Infused Moonshine

- 2 (5-inch-long) pieces of fresh ginger, sliced thinly lengthwise or cut into coins

- 3 cups unflavored moonshine

Using a 1-quart jar, place the ginger slices on the bottom. With a large spoon, crush the ginger. Pour in the moonshine. Seal the jar with a lid. Shake the mixture. Let sit for 1 week, shaking once or twice a day. Using a sieve or coffee filter, strain the ginger-infused moonshine into a new 1-quart jar. Serve immediately or cover and store in freezer for up to 4 months.

Yields approximately 3 cups.

Cocoa Bean-Infused Moonshine

- 2 cups cocoa beans

- 3 cups unflavored moonshine

Using a 1-quart jar, add the cocoa beans. Pour in the moonshine. Seal the jar with a lid. Shake the mixture. Let sit for 5 days to 1 week, shaking once or twice a day. Using a sieve or coffee filter, strain the cocoa bean–infused moonshine into a new 1-quart jar. Serve immediately or cover and store in freezer for up to 2 months.

Yields approximately 3 cups.

Coffee Bean-
Infused Moonshine

- 1 cup coffee beans,
  gently ground or crushed

- 3 cups unflavored moonshine

Using a 1-quart jar, add the coffee beans. Pour in the moonshine. Seal the jar with a lid. Shake the mixture. Let sit for 1 week, shaking once or twice a day. Using a sieve or coffee filter, strain the coffee bean–infused moonshine into a new 1-quart jar. Serve immediately or cover and store in freezer for up to 2 months.

Yields approximately 3 cups.

Vanilla Bean-Infused Moonshine

- 3 to 5 vanilla beans, split down the middle

- 3 cups unflavored moonshine

Using a 1-quart jar, add the vanilla beans. Pour in the moonshine. Seal the jar with a lid. Shake the mixture. Let sit for 1 to 3 weeks, shaking once or twice a day. Using a sieve or coffee filter, strain the vanilla bean–infused moonshine into a new 1-quart jar. Serve immediately or cover and store in freezer for up to 2 months.

Yields approximately 3 cups.

Lavender-Infused Moonshine

- 1 large bunch fresh lavender (15 to 20 stems)

- 3 cups unflavored moonshine

Using a 1-quart jar, add the lavender. Pour in the moonshine. Seal the jar with a lid. Shake the mixture. Let sit for 2 to 3 weeks, shaking once or twice a day. Using a sieve or coffee filter, strain the lavender-infused moonshine into a new 1-quart jar. Serve immediately or cover and store in freezer for up to 1 month.

Yields approximately 3 cups.

Dandelion-Infused Moonshine

- 2 cups freshly picked dandelion flowers, rinsed and stems and green bases removed

- 3 cups unflavored moonshine

Using a 1-quart jar, add the dandelions. Pour in the moonshine. Seal the jar with a lid. Shake the mixture. Let sit for 5 days to 1 week, shaking once or twice a day. Using a sieve or coffee filter, strain the dandelion-infused moonshine into a new 1-quart jar. Serve immediately or cover and store in freezer for up to 1 month.

Yields approximately 3 cups.

Rose Petal-Infused Moonshine

- 2 cups dried rose petals

- 3 cups unflavored moonshine

Using a 1-quart jar, add the rose petals. Pour in the moonshine. Seal the jar with a lid. Shake the mixture. Let sit for 1 to 2 weeks, shaking once or twice a day. Using a sieve or coffee filter, strain the rose petal–infused moonshine into a new 1-quart jar. Serve immediately or cover and store in freezer for up to 1 month.

Yields approximately 3 cups.

Honey-Infused Moonshine

- 1 ½ cups raw honey

- 3 cups unflavored moonshine

Using a 1-quart jar, add the honey. Pour in the moonshine. Seal the jar with a lid. Shake the mixture. Let sit for 3 days to 1 week, shaking once or twice a day. Using a sieve or coffee filter, strain the honey-infused moonshine into a new 1-quart jar. Serve immediately or cover and store in freezer for up to 1 month.

Yields approximately 3 cups.

Pine-Infused Moonshine

- 4 (2 to 3-inch) freshly cut pine sprigs

- 3 cups unflavored moonshine

Using a 1-quart jar, add the pine sprigs. Pour in the moonshine. Seal the jar with a lid. Shake the mixture. Let sit for 3 days to 1 week, shaking once or twice a day. Using a sieve or coffee filter, strain the pine-infused moonshine into a new 1-quart jar. Serve immediately or cover and store in freezer for up to 1 month.

Yields approximately 3 cups.

The Moonshiner's Playlist

If you want to dance to a moonshiner's beat, here is the ultimate playlist of songs about or that mention moonshine.

Dolly Parton's "Daddy's Moonshine Still"
(Written by Dolly Parton)

Willie Nelson's "Good Old Mountain Dew"
(Written by Scotty Wiseman)

Robert Mitchum's "The Ballad of Thunder Road"
(Written by Don Raye and Robert Mitchum as the
title track for his movie *Thunder Road*)

George Jones's "White Lightning"
(Written by J. P. Richardson and also recorded
by Conway Twitty and Waylon Jennings)

"Rocky Top"
(Written by Felice Bryant and Boudleaux Bryant)

Hank Williams III's "Moonshiner's Life"
(Written by Hank Williams III)

Joan Baez's "Copper Kettle"
(Written by Albert Frank Beddoe)

Florida Georgia Line's "Get Your Shine On"
(Written by Brian Kelley, Tyler Hubbard,
Rodney Clawson, and Chris Tompkins)

Jake Owen's "Apple Pie Moonshine"
(Written by Rodney Clawson, Chris Tompkins,
Chad Kroeger, and Craig Wiseman)

Brad Paisley's album and title song "Moonshine in the Trunk"
(Written by Brad Paisley, Brent Anderson, and Chris DuBois)

Cissie Lynn's and Doug Kershaw's "The Butcher Holler
Moonshine Song: Thunder on the Mountain"

New Lost City Ramblers' album
American Moonshine and Prohibition
(This compilation of seventeen tracks includes: "Drunkard's Hic-
cups," "Bootlegger's Story," "The Moonshiner," "Old Homebrew,"
"Whiskey Seller," "Prohibition Is a Failure," "The Teetotals,"
"Wreck on the Highway," "Al Smith for President," and "Down to
the Stillhouse to Get a Litter Cider.")

The Grateful Dead's "Brown-Eyed Women"
(Written by Jerry Garcia and Robert Hunter)

George Clinton's Funk band Parliament's "Moonshine Heather"
(Written by George Clinton)

Beach Boy Dennis Wilson's "Moonshine"
(Written by Dennis Wilson and Gregg Jakobson)

Metallica's "Whiskey in the Jar"
(Written by Eric Bell, Brian Downey, and Phil Lynott)

Aerosmith's "Rag Doll"
(Written by Steven Tyler, Joe Perry, Jim Vallance, and Holly Knight)

Candy and Moonshine Infusions

Peppermint Candy-Infused Moonshine

- 8 to 10 peppermint candy canes or 12 to 17 small round peppermint candies, crushed

- 3 cups unflavored moonshine

Using a 1-quart jar, add the peppermint candy. Pour in the moonshine. Seal the jar with a lid. Shake the mixture. Let sit for 3 days to 1 week, shaking once or twice a day. Using a sieve or coffee filter, strain the peppermint candy–infused moonshine into a new 1-quart jar. Serve immediately or cover and store in freezer for up to 1 month.

Yields approximately 3 cups.

Jelly Bean-Infused Moonshine

- 2 cups jelly beans of choice
  (single flavor or multi flavors)

- 3 cups unflavored moonshine

Using a 1-quart jar, add the jelly beans. Pour in the moonshine. Seal the jar with a lid. Shake the mixture. Let sit for 3 days to 1 week, shaking once or twice a day. Using a sieve or coffee filter, strain the jelly bean–infused moonshine into a new 1-quart jar. Serve immediately or cover and store in freezer for up to 1 month.

Yields approximately 3 cups.

Bubble Gum-Infused Moonshine

- 20 pieces of bubble gum, cut into small pieces

- 3 cups unflavored moonshine

Using a 1-quart jar, add the bubble gum. Pour in the moonshine. Seal the jar with a lid. Shake the mixture. Let sit for 2 to 5 days, shaking once or twice a day. Using a sieve or coffee filter, strain the bubble gum–infused moonshine into a new 1-quart jar. Serve immediately or cover and store in freezer for up to 1 month.

Yields approximately 3 cups.

Marshmallow-Infused Moonshine

- 2 cups small marshmallows, halved, or 2 cups sliced large marshmallows

- 3 cups unflavored moonshine

Using a 1-quart jar, add the marshmallows. Pour in the moonshine. Seal the jar with a lid. Shake the mixture. Let sit for 3 days to 1 week, shaking once or twice a day. Using a sieve or coffee filter, strain the marshmallow-infused moonshine into a new 1-quart jar. Serve immediately or cover and store in freezer for up to 1 month.

Yields approximately 3 cups.

Gummy Candy-Infused Moonshine

- 2 cups gummy candy of choice

- 3 cups unflavored moonshine

Using a 1-quart jar, add the gummy candy. Pour in the moonshine. Seal the jar with a lid. Shake the mixture. Let sit for 2 to 3 days, shaking once or twice a day. Using a sieve or coffee filter, strain the gummy candy–infused moonshine into a new 1-quart jar, and place the moonshine-infused gummy candy into a separate jar to enjoy. Serve the moonshine immediately or cover and store in freezer for up to 1 month. Serve the gummy candy immediately.

Yields approximately 3 cups.

Skittles®-Infused Moonshine

- 2 cups Skittles® of choice by flavor

- 3 cups unflavored moonshine

Using a 1-quart jar, add the Skittles. Pour in the moonshine. Seal the jar with a lid. Shake the mixture. Let sit for 1 to 2 days, shaking once or twice a day. Using a sieve or coffee filter, strain the Skittles-infused moonshine into a new 1-quart jar. Serve immediately or cover and store in freezer for up to 1 month.

Yields approximately 3 cups.

Butterscotch-
Infused Moonshine

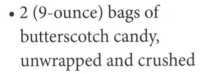

- 2 (9-ounce) bags of butterscotch candy, unwrapped and crushed

- 3 cups unflavored moonshine

Using a 1-quart jar, add the butterscotch candy. Pour in the moonshine. Seal the jar with a lid. Shake the mixture. Let sit for 3 days to 1 week, shaking once or twice a day. Using a sieve or coffee filter, strain the butterscotch-infused moonshine into a new 1-quart jar. Serve immediately or cover and store in freezer for up to 1 month.

Yields approximately 3 cups.

CHAPTER 11

The Moonshiner's Happy Hour

Moonshine Monkey

For sunny backyard parties or holidays year-round, this pineapple-infused moonshine, amaretto, and rum punch will inspire your wild side to let the good times roll.

- 8 ounces unflavored or pineapple-infused moonshine (p. 111)
- 5 ounces amaretto
- 5 ounces rum
- 24 ounces ginger ale
- 12 ounces orange juice
- 12 ounces pineapple juice
- Ice

In a large punch bowl, combine all the ingredients, stirring well. Serve chilled in Mason jars.

Yields 12 to 15 cocktails.

Happy Sally's Sweet Tea

Two of the South's most popular staples—tea and moonshine—conspire to indulge your sweet tooth with every sip.

- 3 cups boiling water
- 8 tea bags
- 1 cup sugar, or more to taste
- 5 cups cool water
- 1 to 2 cups unflavored or peach-infused moonshine (p. 112), or to taste

In a large glass pitcher, add the boiling water and tea bags. Let steep for 30 minutes. Then remove the tea bags. Add the sugar, stirring until dissolved. Add the cool water, stirring. Refrigerate for 1 to 2 hours, or until cold. Add the moonshine, mixing well. Serve in tall Mason jars over the rocks.

Yields 8 cocktails.

The Bootlegger's Navel

This rebel's twist on a classic—with its trio of moonshine, peach schnapps, and OJ—will keep the party flowing from brunch to sundown, and beyond.

- ½ ounce unflavored or peach-infused moonshine (p. 112)
- ½ ounce peach schnapps
- Orange juice

In a Mason jar filled halfway with ice cubes, combine the moonshine and peach schnapps. Fill the remainder of the jar with the orange juice, stirring well.

Yields 1 cocktail.

The Moonshiner's Slushy

Moonshine transforms this strawberry-orange slush into an icy treat that works as both a holiday party starter and a sunny day refresher.

- 1 (.16-ounce) packet strawberry Kool-Aid®, or other strawberry flavored powdered drink mix
- 3 cups sugar
- 8 ounces orange juice
- 4 ½ cups warm water
- 1 ½ cups unflavored or strawberry-infused moonshine (p. 129)
- 10 ounces fresh strawberries, halved or sliced
- 1 to 2 large oranges, peeled and cut into small chunks
- Ginger ale, to taste

In a large saucepan over medium heat, combine the Kool-Aid, sugar, orange juice, and warm water. Stir until the Kool-Aid and sugar are dissolved. Remove from the heat. Add the moonshine, strawberries, and oranges, stirring. Pour the mixture into a large container, cover, and freeze overnight. To serve, scoop the slush into Mason jars, filling them halfway or more. Then add the ginger ale to taste.

Yields 10 to 12 cocktails.

Mountain Julep

The traditional mint julep gets supercharged with a little white lightning to insure every jarful is a triple crown winner.

- 5 fresh mint leaves
- 1 ounce simple syrup
- Crushed ice
- 3 ounces unflavored or mint-infused moonshine (p. 158)
- Splash of water
- 1 fresh mint sprig (for garnishing)

In a Mason jar, combine and muddle the mint leaves and simple syrup. Add the crushed ice. Pour in the moonshine. Add the splash of water. Add more ice, if desired. Garnish with the mint sprig.

Yields 1 cocktail.

Appalachian Watermelon Martini

A few rounds of these watermelon, pineapple, and moonshine martinis will spike your fun with family and friends to all new heights.

- 5 ounces store-bought or freshly blended (seeds removed) watermelon juice
- 2 ounces unflavored or watermelon-infused moonshine (p. 115)
- 2 ounces pineapple juice
- Watermelon cubes and fresh or frozen berries of choice (for garnishing)

In a shaker filled with ice, combine all the ingredients, except the garnishes, shaking. Strain the cocktail into a Mason jar. Add the watermelon cubes and berries on skewers or as floating garnishes.

Yields 1 cocktail.

Apple Moon Cider

Whether kicking back with friends by the light of a harvest moon or winding your way through a corn maze, this moonshine-infused apple cider will make those breezy days of autumn all the brighter.

- 1 gallon apple juice
- 1 gallon apple cider
- 4 cups sugar
- 10 cinnamon sticks
- 3 cups unflavored or apple pie–flavored moonshine, or Old Apple Tree Likker (p. 119)

In a large pot, combine all the ingredients, except the moonshine. Bring the mixture to a boil, stirring several times. Remove from the heat. Cool completely. Stir in the moonshine, mixing well. Serve reheated or chilled over the rocks in Mason jars.

Yields 40 cocktails.

The Thorpe

Inspired by the classic Stinger and in tribute to the first American colonist to distill corn whiskey in 1620, this smooth blend of brandy, crème de menthe, and mint-infused moonshine is a sophisticated refresher that's perfect for after dinner or as an any-time sipper.

- 1 shot brandy
- 1 shot white crème de menthe
- 1 shot mint-infused moonshine (p. 158)

Fill a small Mason jar with ice (cubes or crushed). Pour in each shot and stir to combine. Add more ice to fill the glass. Serve very cold.

Yields 1 cocktail.

The Whiskey Rebel's Daiquiri

There are daiquiris, and then there are daiquiris. Any whiskey rebel worth his or her weight in fun will enjoy how the strawberry-infused moonshine in this icy thirst quencher brings sparks of pure delight to any occasion. And don't be shy about adding a banana, blueberries, or other fruits to the mix.

- 5 cups crushed ice
- 1 ½ cups rum
- 2 ounces strawberry-infused moonshine (p. 129)
- ¾ cup fresh lime juice
- ½ cup fresh lemon juice
- ½ cup sugar
- 1 (16-ounce) package frozen whole strawberries
- Fresh or moonshine-infused strawberries (p. 129) (for garnishing)

In a blender, combine the ice, rum, moonshine, lime juice, lemon juice, and sugar, blending until the sugar is dissolved. Continue to blend, adding a few frozen strawberries at a time, until smooth. Serve in tall, chilled Mason jars. Garnish with the strawberries on skewers.

Yields 6 to 8 cocktails.

Summer Tripper

No matter the time of year you serve it, this cranberry-infused moonshine and peach schnapps cocktail is always summer in a Mason jar.

- 1 ounce unflavored or cranberry-infused moonshine (p. 132)
- 1 ounce peach schnapps
- 1 ounce cranberry juice
- 1 ounce pineapple juice
- 1 ounce orange juice

In a shaker filled with ice, combine all the ingredients, shaking well. Strain into a Mason jar.

Yields 1 cocktail.

Dirt Road Colada

When pineapple- or coconut-infused moonshine meets the rum in this amplified piña colada, you'll discover why moonshiners have long seen their dirt road kingdoms as nothing but pure paradise.

- 2 ounces rum
- 2 ounces cream of coconut
- 1 ounce coconut milk
- 1 ounce pineapple-infused moonshine (p. 111) or coconut-infused moonshine (p. 125)
- 2 ounces pineapple juice
- 1 cup crushed ice
- Slices or cubes of regular or moonshine-infused pineapple (for garnishing) (p. 111)
- Regular or moonshine-infused maraschino cherries (for garnishing) (p. 118)

In a blender, combine all the ingredients, except the pineapple slices and maraschino cherries. Blend until smooth. Serve in a tall, chilled Mason jar. Garnish with the pineapple and cherries.

Yields 1 cocktail.

Wild Rose

A wild rose by any other name . . . is just as scrumptious in this rose petal–infused moonshine cocktail with freshly made rose petal syrup.

- 3 ounces rose petal–infused moonshine (p. 167)
- ½ to 1 ounce cranberry juice or club soda
- 1 ounce rose petal syrup (recipe p. 197) (optional, but recommended)
- Rose petals (for garnishing)

In a shaker filled with ice, combine the moonshine, cranberry juice or club soda, and rose petal syrup, shaking well. Strain into a Mason jar. Garnish with the rose petals.

Yields 1 cocktail.

Rose Petal Syrup

- ½ cup sugar
- 3 teaspoons dried rose petals
- 1 cup water

In a small mortar or bowl, combine the sugar and rose petals. Using a pestle, crush the rose petals into the sugar. In a small saucepan, combine the sugar and rose petal mixture with the water. Bring the mixture to a simmer, stirring until the sugar dissolves, about 3 minutes. Cool the mixture.

Party in the Holler

No matter where you call home, you can always party like a moonshiner with this high-octane fruit punch fueled by rum, amaretto, gin, beer, and white lightning.

- 1 quart rum
- 1 quart unflavored moonshine or fruit-infused moonshine of choice, such as orange (p. 114), banana (p. 124), peach (p. 112), or pineapple (p. 111)
- 1 quart amaretto
- 1 quart gin
- ½ quart beer
- 1 can ginger ale
- 1 quart orange juice
- 1 quart pineapple juice
- 1 quart peach juice
- Ice cubes or ice ring

In a large punch bowl, combine all the ingredients, mixing well. Serve on the rocks in Mason jars.

Yields 25 to 30 servings.

Old Apple Tree Likker

There's nothing more American than apple pie and moonshine. Here, you get the best of both with this homemade apple pie moonshine recipe that's easy to make and even easier to send down the ole hatch.

- 3 quarts apple cider
- 3 quarts apple juice
- 2 ½ cups sugar
- 2 tablespoons brown sugar
- 1 teaspoon apple pie spice
- 7 cinnamon sticks
- 1 quart unflavored or apple-infused moonshine (p. 119)

In a large pot over medium heat, combine all the ingredients, except the moonshine. Bring the mixture to a boil, then remove from the heat. Let the mixture cool. Stir in the moonshine. Pour the mixture into 7 (1-quart) Mason jars and seal. Let sit for 1 week or more.

Yields 7 quarts.

Shinny Mary

This moonshine-infused Bloody Mary is one spicy, hot rebel that promises to turn breakfast, brunch, or any get-together on its head. Experiment with a savory moonshine infusion such as jalapeño, peppered celery, horseradish, or leek.

- 8 ounces tomato juice or V8® Spicy Hot
- Splash of Frank's RedHot® Cayenne Pepper Sauce
- Splash of Worcestershire sauce
- ½ teaspoon Sriracha
- 4 ounces unflavored moonshine or infused moonshine of choice, such as jalapeño (p. 138), peppered celery (p. 139), horseradish (p. 142), tomato (p. 143), garlic (p. 140), or leek (p. 146)
- ½ teaspoon horseradish, or to taste
- Seasoned salt, to taste
- Pepper, to taste
- Celery stalk
- Green onion

In a tall, chilled Mason jar, combine all the ingredients over the rocks, adding the seasoning to taste. Garnish with the celery and onion.

Yields 1 cocktail.

Speakeasy

This lemony moonshine cocktail has all the style and flare you'll need to bring the carefree, party-the-night away attitude of the speakeasy to your next happy hour.

- 3 cups lemon-infused moonshine (p. 116)
- ¾ cup freshly squeezed lemon juice
- ¾ cup sugar
- 4 to 6 lemon wedges (for garnishing)

In a shaker filled with ice, combine all the ingredients, except the lemon wedges. Shake well to combine. Strain into Mason jars and garnish with the lemon wedges.

Yields 4 to 6 cocktails.

The Naughty Plum

The humble (and vastly underrated) plum gets its shining moment in this white lightning and Prosecco cocktail that is reminiscent of a mimosa, but definitely marches to its own beat.

- 1 plum, halved, pitted, and chopped
- 1 ounce simple syrup
- 2 ounces plum-infused moonshine (p. 120)
- Prosecco, chilled

In a blender, combine the plum and simple syrup, blending until smooth. Add the moonshine, blending to mix. Divide the mixture in two chilled Mason jars. Fill the jars with the Prosecco.

Yields 2 cocktails.

Moonshine Mule

Lime-infused moonshine ensures that this rebellious takeover of the Moscow Mule delivers a real kick of spirit and buzz.

- 1 ounce unflavored or lime-infused moonshine (p. 116)
- 4 ounces ginger beer
- Juice from ½ lime
- Slice of fresh lime (for garnishing)

Fill a small Mason jar with ice. Add the moonshine, ginger beer, and lime juice, stirring to combine. Garnish with the lime slice.

Yields 1 cocktail.

Virginia Pear Mimosa

Pear-infused moonshine adds an unexpected twist to the brunch mimosa, making it perfect for toasts to great friends and good living.

- 2 ounces pear-infused moonshine (p. 117)
- 1 ounce orange or mango juice
- Champagne
- 1 pear wedge (for garnishing)

In a chilled Mason jar, combine the moonshine and orange juice. Fill the remainder of the jar with champagne. Garnish with the pear wedge.

Yields 1 cocktail.

Smokey Mountain S'more

The classic, most beloved campfire treat of all time just got a moonshine makeover! Whether savored fireside or not, marshmallow-infused moonshine and chocolate liqueur prove that indulging your sweet tooth doesn't get any better than this.

- Powdered cocoa on a small plate (for rimming the Mason jar)
- 2 ounces marshmallow-infused moonshine (p. 176)
- 1 ½ ounces chocolate liqueur
- Chocolate syrup (for drizzling) (optional, but recommended)
- 5 small marshmallows
- 1 small (bite-size) chocolate bar
- Graham crackers

Moisten the rim of a small Mason jar with water. Then press the rim into the cocoa. In a shaker filled with ice, combine the moonshine and liqueur, shaking well. Strain into the Mason jar. Drizzle with chocolate syrup, if desired. Garnish with the marshmallows and chocolate bar on a skewer laid across the top of the rim. Serve graham crackers on the side.

Yields 1 cocktail.

Hillbilly Berry Bush

This fresh berry-infused moonshine cocktail is your perfect excuse to hit up the countryside and go berry picking come summer. The mix-and-match moonshine and berry options present endless combinations for a different party starter every time.

- 2 cups fresh berries, such as strawberry, blackberry, blueberry, or raspberry
- 4 cups berry-infused moonshine, such as strawberry (p. 129), blackberry (p. 130), blueberry (p. 128), or raspberry (p. 131)
- 4 tablespoons freshly squeezed lemon juice
- 4 tablespoons freshly squeezed lime juice
- 2 tablespoons sugar
- Club soda, to taste
- Fresh berries (for garnishing)

In a shaker, combine all the ingredients (matching fresh berries to the berry-infused moonshine being used), except the club soda and berries for garnishing. Muddle the berries. Shake well to combine. Strain into Mason jars on the rocks. Add the club soda, stirring to combine. Garnish with fresh berries on a skewer.

Yields 4 cocktails.

Peppermint Lightning

Custom-made for the holiday season, peppermint candy–infused moonshine combined with white crème de menthe and vanilla extract will make all your get-togethers merry and bright, regardless of if you've been naughty or nice.

- 5 ounces peppermint candy–infused moonshine (p. 173)
- 1 ounce white crème de menthe
- 1 tablespoon vanilla extract, or to taste
- 2 peppermint sticks (for garnishing)

In a shaker filled with ice, combine all the ingredients, except the peppermint sticks, shaking well. Strain into Mason jars, on the rocks, if desired. Garnish with the peppermint sticks.

Yields 2 cocktails.

Basil Shiner

Basil's aromatic notes of pepper, mint, and anise in both the fresh leaves and moonshine infusion complement the dance of tart and sweet juice flavors to compose an unforgettable quencher.

- 5 fresh basil leaves
- 1 ounce simple syrup
- Juice from 1 lemon
- Juice from ½ lime
- Juice from ½ small orange
- 3 ounces basil-infused moonshine (p. 153)
- 1 lemon slice (for garnishing)

In a shaker, combine all the ingredients, except the moonshine and garnish. Muddle the basil leaves. Add crushed ice. Add the moonshine, shaking well. Strain into a chilled Mason jar. Garnish with the lemon slice.

Yields 1 cocktail.

Kentucky Honey Bee

Sweet and spicy, and oh so cozy, the honey-infused moonshine, rum, and apple juice here will warm your heart and make your smile grow with every round.

- 2 ounces honey-infused moonshine (p. 168)
- 1 ounce spiced rum
- 3 ounces apple juice
- 1 tablespoon honey

In a shaker filled with ice, combine all the ingredients, shaking well. Strain into a Mason jar over the rocks.

Yields 1 cocktail.

Lemongrass and Mint Mojito

For all those long and lazy afternoons, this cool coupling of lemongrass- and mint-infused moonshines will help you kick back with friends and watch the rest of the world pass right on by.

- ½ cup mint leaves
- ½ cup simple syrup
- ½ cup lemongrass-infused moonshine (p. 154)
- ½ cup mint-infused moonshine (p. 158)
- 1 ½ cups club soda, chilled
- 4 stalks of lemongrass (for garnishing)

In a shaker, gently muddle the mint leaves. Fill with ice. Add the remaining ingredients, except the lemongrass stalks, shaking well. Strain into chilled Mason jars. Garnish with the lemongrass stalks.

Yields 4 cocktails.

Redneck Knockout

Fruit-infused moonshine, beer, and juices pack a punch of buzz and flavor that will set your inner redneck free to party the night away without a care in the world.

- 3 quarts unflavored or fruit-infused moonshine, such as lemon (p. 116) or strawberry (p. 129)
- 2 quarts beer, such as American Lager, American Amber, or Hefeweizen
- 4 quarts lemonade concentrate
- 3 quarts water
- 3 quarts fruit punch
- Ice ring
- Fresh strawberries, raspberries, blueberries, and any other berries of choice (for garnishing)

In a large punch bowl, combine all the ingredients, except the ice and fresh berries, stirring well. Add the ice ring and berries. Serve over the rocks in Mason jars.

Yields 25 to 30 servings.

Old Horsey

This new spin on an Old Fashioned—with orange-infused white lighting and moonshine-soaked maraschino cherries—will always be in style and on trend for any occasion.

- 3 dashes bitters
- 1 ½ teaspoons water
- 2 ½ teaspoons simple syrup
- Ice cubes
- 2 ounces orange-infused moonshine (p. 114)
- 1 orange wedge (for garnishing)
- 2 regular or moonshine-infused maraschino cherries (for garnishing) (p. 118)

In a Mason jar, combine the bitters, water, and simple syrup, stirring to combine. Add the ice cubes. Add the moonshine, stirring to combine. Garnish with the orange wedge and cherries on a skewer.

Yields 1 cocktail.

Rise 'N Shine Sazerac

The licorice notes of anise in both the liqueur and infused moonshine combined with the sweet accent of Peychaud's Bitters will happily take your taste buds off the beaten path.

- ½ teaspoon anise-flavored liqueur
- ½ teaspoon sugar
- 1 tablespoon water
- Peychaud's® Aromatic Cocktail Bitters, to taste
- ½ cup unflavored or anise-infused moonshine (p. 156)
- 1 lemon wedge (for garnishing)

Using a chilled Mason jar, swirl the anise-flavored liqueur around the inside, and then pour out. In the Mason jar, combine the sugar, water, and bitters, stirring until dissolved. Add the moonshine, stirring to combine. Garnish with the lemon wedge.

Yields 1 cocktail.

Blue Ridge Toddy

Nothing goes better with curling up under a blanket on a chilly day than this warm and cozy apple pie moonshine toddy.

- 3 ounces boiling water
- 2 ounces unflavored or apple pie moonshine, or Old Apple Tree Likker (p. 119)
- 1 ½ teaspoons honey
- 2 whole cloves
- 2 cinnamon sticks
- Juice from ½ lemon
- 1 pinch ground nutmeg

In a Mason jar, combine the water, moonshine, and honey, stirring to combine. Add the cloves, cinnamon sticks, lemon juice, and nutmeg. Mix well. Serve warm.

Yields 1 cocktail.

Stockcar

A bootlegger's reimagining of the swanky Sidecar, straight moonshine added to Cointreau, lemon juice, and cognac will rev up your engines for chasing down a great time from one mountaintop to the next.

- 1 ounce Cointreau
- ¾ ounce lemon juice
- ½ ounce cognac
- 1 ounce unflavored moonshine
- Lemon slice (for garnishing)

In a shaker filled with ice, combine all the ingredients, except the lemon slice, shaking well. Strain into a Mason jar. Garnish with the lemon slice.

Yields 1 cocktail.

XXX Shine 'N Shake

Some things are not too good to be true. Like ice cream and moonshine in one Mason jar! Your choice of vanilla bean– or cocoa bean–infused XXX, and vanilla or chocolate ice cream provide multiple options for a milk shake that will blow your mind. And the cherry on top of this delicious treat time is literally a moonshine-infused cherry on top!

- 3 ounces unflavored moonshine, vanilla bean–infused moonshine (p. 164), or cocoa bean–infused moonshine (p. 162)
- 2 ½ cups Kahlua
- 2 ½ cups vanilla or chocolate almond milk
- ½ cup tonic water
- 1 teaspoon pure vanilla extract
- 5 cups vanilla or chocolate ice cream
- Regular or moonshine-infused maraschino cherries (for garnishing) (p. 118)

In a blender, combine all the ingredients, except the cherries, blending until smooth. Pour into chilled Mason jars. Garnish with the cherries.

Yields 4 to 5 servings.

Nutty Moonshiner

The sweet almond tones of the amaretto and rum get an extra power boost of nuttiness from the almond-infused moonshine for a perfect pre-dinner cocktail between friends, be they from across the street or the other end of the holler.

- 1 ounce nut-flavored moonshine, such as Nutty-Infused Moonshine using almonds (p. 127)
- 2 ounces amaretto
- 1 ounce rum

In a Mason jar filled with crushed ice, add all the ingredients, stirring to combine.

Yields 1 cocktail.

The 180

Sipping this threesome of straight-up moonshine, Southern Comfort, and American Amber Lager will leave you spinning for joy.

- 2 ounces unflavored moonshine
- 4 ounces Southern Comfort
- 12 ounces American Amber Lager

In a pitcher, add all the ingredients, stirring to combine. Pour into Mason jars filled with ice.

Yields 2 to 4 cocktails.

Howl at the Moon

These are the specific instructions for enjoying this shot that mingles tequila, lime-infused moonshine, and agave nectar: Raise a toast to the moon, drink fast, and commence howling!

- 2 ounces tequila
- 1 ounce lime-infused moonshine (p. 116)
- Juice from 1 lime
- 2 tablespoons agave nectar

In a shot glass, add all the ingredients, stirring to combine.

Yields 1 shot.

Creek Breeze

Every moonshiner knows there's nothing like the cool, invigorating breeze that winds its way down along mountain creeks, which have long provided many of them with one of the main ingredients for their white lightning. The only thing that could make time along the creek even better is this juicy cranberry-infused moonshine reincarnation of the Sea Breeze.

- 2 ounces unflavored or cranberry-infused moonshine (p. 132)
- 6 ounces cranberry juice
- 2 ounces grapefruit juice
- ½ ounce fresh lime juice
- Splash of fresh creek water (optional, but recommended)

In a Mason jar filled halfway with ice cubes, combine all the ingredients, stirring well.

Yields 1 to 2 cocktails.

Yell-O Moon Shots

It's not a party until the gelatin shots arrive. In this moonshiner's version, the duo of homemade fruit- or berry-infused moonshine and coconut milk is so delicious that you may even choose to serve larger portions topped with whipped cream as an indulgent snack or dessert.

- 1 cup water
- 1 cup coconut milk
- 1 (3-ounce) packet gelatin, unflavored or flavored
- 1 cup fruit- or berry-flavored moonshine, such as peach (p. 112), banana (p. 124), strawberry (p. 129), or blueberry (p. 128)

In a medium-size pan, combine the water and coconut milk. Bring the mixture to a boil. Add ½ packet of gelatin, stirring to dissolve. Add the moonshine, stirring. Divide the mixture among 8 (2-ounce) cups. Refrigerate the cups until the gelatin has set, several hours to overnight. Serve chilled.

Yields 8 shots.

Banana Split

This moonshiner's banana split cocktail made with banana-infused moonshine and served with all the trimmings—chocolate syrup, coconut flakes, and chocolate shavings—is the ideal way to indulge the craving to have your dessert and drink it, too.

- 1 ounce banana liqueur
- 1 ounce banana-infused moonshine (p. 124)
- ½ cup vanilla or coconut milk
- 1 ½ cups crushed ice
- 1 tablespoon chocolate syrup
- Coconut flakes (for garnishing)
- Chocolate shavings (for garnishing)

In a shaker, combine all the ingredients, except the chocolate syrup and garnishes, shaking well. Strain into a Mason jar. Drizzle the chocolate on top and sprinkle with the coconut flakes and chocolate shavings.

Yields 1 cocktail.

Lavender Wildcat

If you really, really want to dazzle your guests, this lavender-infused moonshine cocktail with freshly made lavender syrup will do the trick to the tune of its lightly sweet and floral 90-proof notes.

- 2 ounces lavender-infused moonshine (p. 165)
- ½ ounce freshly squeezed lemon juice
- 1 ounce lavender syrup (recipe p. 229) (optional, but recommended)
- 1 fresh lavender sprig (for garnishing)

In a shaker filled with ice, combine the moonshine, lemon juice, and lavender syrup, shaking well. Strain into a Mason jar. Garnish with the lavender sprig.

Yields 1 cocktail.

Lavender Syrup

- ½ cup sugar
- 3 teaspoons dried lavender
- 1 cup water

In a small mortar or bowl, combine the sugar and lavender. Using a pestle, crush the lavender into the sugar. In a small saucepan, combine the sugar and lavender mixture with the water. Bring the mixture to a simmer, stirring until the sugar dissolves, about 3 minutes. Cool the mixture.

Moonshine Rita

The iconic margarita gets infused with a dose of pure Appalachian magic complements of orange-infused moonshine and maraschino cherries that have been soaked in hooch.

- ½ fresh lime
- Salt on a small plate (for salting the rims of the Mason jars)
- 2 cups sweet and sour mix
- 1 ½ cups triple sec
- 1 ½ cups tequila
- ½ cup orange liqueur
- ½ cup unflavored or orange-infused moonshine (p. 114)
- 8 fresh lime wedges (for garnishing)
- Regular or moonshine-infused maraschino cherries (for garnishing) (p. 118)

Rub the rims of 6 to 8 chilled Mason jars with the lime. Then press the rims into the salt. Fill the glasses with ice (cubes or crushed). In a blender, combine the remaining ingredients, except the lime wedges and cherries, blending until smooth. Serve in the Mason jars and garnish each with a lime wedge and maraschino cherry.

Yields 6 to 8 cocktails.

Twenty-first Amendment

If ever there was an occasion to raise a toast, it was when Prohibition was repealed by the Twenty-first Amendment to the U.S. Constitution. In tribute, this moonshiner's sangria lets you offer a tipsy patriot's salute with four—four!!!—different fruity moonshine infusions.

- 2 quarts apple pie moonshine or Old Apple Tree Likker (p. 119)
- ½ quart orange-infused moonshine (p. 114)
- ½ quart peach-infused moonshine (p. 112)
- ½ quart strawberry-infused moonshine (p. 129)
- 1 quart red wine
- ½ quart triple sec
- 3 quarts orange juice
- 1 (16-ounce) package of fresh strawberries
- 3 cups blueberries
- 3 cups grapes
- 5 large peaches, quartered
- 5 large oranges, peeled and quartered
- 5 large apples, peeled and quartered
- Ice cubes or ice ring

In a large punch bowl, combine all the ingredients, mixing well. Serve on the rocks in Mason jars.

Yields 25 to 30 servings.

Tipsy Dandelion Smoothie

Dandelion-infused moonshine blended with vanilla almond milk, coconut oil, honey, and a crop of fresh bananas, blueberries, and strawberries offers a boozy smoothie that is packed full of vitamins and buzz.

- ½ cup water
- 1 cup crushed ice
- ½ cup dandelion-infused moonshine (p. 166)
- 1 small fresh banana, cut into chunks
- 1 cup fresh or frozen blueberries
- 1 cup fresh or frozen strawberries
- 1 cup fresh dandelion greens, chopped (optional)
- ½ teaspoon coconut oil
- ½ cup vanilla almond or coconut milk
- ½ teaspoon honey

In a blender, combine all the ingredients, blending until smooth. Pour into chilled Mason jars.

Yields 2 to 4 cocktails.

The Peppered Celery

Clean and wholesome, celery finally gets the headlining credit it deserves in this peppery moonshine cocktail that has all the bite you want, and more, thanks to the muddled cilantro and fresh lime juice.

- 3 ounces peppered celery–infused moonshine (p. 139)
- 3 small pieces of celery
- ½ cup cilantro
- 1 ounce freshly squeezed lime juice
- Pinch of pepper
- Tall celery stick (for garnishing)

In a shaker, combine the celery and cilantro, muddling them together. Add the remaining ingredients, except the tall celery stick. Add ice. Shake well. Strain into a Mason jar filled with ice. Garnish with the tall celery stick.

Yields 1 cocktail.

Tennessee Highball

One of the fastest and easiest moonshine cocktails to whip up, this XXX Highball works inside and outside, as a party starter or for unexpected guests.

- 1 ounce unflavored moonshine or lemon lime–infused moonshine (p. 116)
- 4 to 6 ounces ginger ale, or to taste
- 1 lemon or lime wedge

Pour the moonshine into a Mason jar with ice cubes. Add the ginger ale. Garnish with the lemon or lime wedge.

Yields 1 cocktail.

The Moonrunner's Manhattan

Struck with a little white lightning, this revamped Manhattan is high proof that moonshine—especially cherry-infused, including a hooch-soaked maraschino cherry—can even make perfection a little more perfect.

- 1 ½ ounces cherry-infused moonshine (p. 118)
- ¾ ounce dry or sweet vermouth
- 1 dash Angostura® Aromatic Bitters
- 1 dash simple syrup
- 1 teaspoon maraschino cherry juice, or to taste
- Lemon slice (for garnishing)
- Regular or moonshine-infused maraschino cherries (for garnishing) (p. 118)

In a small Mason jar with ice cubes, add all of the ingredients, except the garnish, stirring to combine. Garnish with the lemon slice and cherries.

Yields 1 cocktail.

Moonshine Joe

Make your coffee breaks all the more decadent by adding coffee-infused moonshine—or even the cocoa bean or vanilla bean versions—and a heap of whipped cream to your next cup of Joe.

- 1 ounce coffee-infused moonshine (p. 163), or other infused moonshine of choice, such as cocoa bean (p. 162) or vanilla bean (p. 164)
- 3 to 5 ounces hot coffee
- 1 teaspoon sugar, or to taste
- Whipped cream

In a Mason jar with a handle, combine the moonshine, coffee, and sugar, stirring well. Top with the whipped cream.

Yields 1 serving.

Copper Still

This triple blast of Scotch, moonshine, and Drambuie—with its blend of herb, spice, and honey notes—is the best way to reward yourself anytime you want.

- 1 ½ ounces Scotch
- ½ ounce unflavored moonshine
- ¾ ounce Drambuie
- 1 dash of Angostura® Aromatic Bitters

In a Mason jar with ice cubes, combine all the ingredients, stirring well.

Yields 1 cocktail.

Salty Bow-Wow

Man's best friend just became everyone's best friend in this moonshine homage to the traditional Salty Dog by using grapefruit-infused white lightning to up the ante for any celebration, great or small.

- 1 teaspoon salt on a small plate (for salting the rim)
- 2 ounces grapefruit-infused moonshine (p. 113)
- 6 ounces grapefruit juice
- Club soda, to taste (optional)

Moisten the rim of a Mason jar with water. Dip the rim in the salt. In the Mason jar, combine the moonshine and grapefruit juice, and club soda, if desired. Stir to combine. Add ice.

Yields 1 cocktail.

Spiked Georgia Peach

Sweet, juicy peaches just make life a little better all around. And when peach-infused moonshine is involved for this backwoods-inspired bellini, the sky is the limit for living life to the fullest.

- 2 ounces peach puree or juice
- 2 ounces peach-infused moonshine (p. 112)
- Champagne or Prosecco, chilled

In a chilled Mason jar, combine the peach puree or juice and moonshine, stirring to combine. Fill the remainder of the jar with the champagne.

Yields 1 cocktail.

The Catdaddy

Straight-up hooch, fresh lemon juice, lemon liqueur, and elderflower cordial will give you a moonshiner's swagger with every tangy, sweet sip.

- 2 ounces unflavored moonshine
- ½ ounce freshly squeezed lemon juice
- ½ ounce lemon liqueur
- 1 ounce elderflower cordial
- Club soda

In a shaker filled with ice, combine all the ingredients, except the club soda, shaking well. Strain into a Mason jar. Add the club soda to taste.

Yields 1 cocktail.

Carolina Dillbilly

Dill pickles go from burger sidekick to main attraction in this dill pickle–infused moonshine martini that works equally well before, during, or after dinner.

- 2 dill pickle spears, cut into chunks
- 5 ounces dill pickle-infused moonshine (p. 144)
- 3 ounces dill pickle juice, or to taste
- 2 dill pickle spears and/or cucumber slices (for garnishing)

In a cocktail shaker, muddle the dill pickle chunks. Add ice. Add the moonshine and dill pickle juice. Shake well. Strain into Mason jars. Garnish with the dill pickle spears.

Yields 2 cocktails.

The Moonshiner's Candy Store

You're about to find out what it's like being a moonshiner in a candy store! When you play around with these combinations of candy-infused XXX, the result will be a party punch that is anything but childish.

- 1 quart pink lemonade or cherry Kool-Aid®, or other flavors of choice
- ¼ quart candy-infused moonshine, such as Skittles® (p. 178), gummy candy (p. 177), jelly bean (p. 174), or bubble gum (p. 175)
- 16 ounces ginger ale, chilled
- Garnishes of choice: Skittles®, gummy candy, or jelly beans

In a small punch bowl or other container, combine all the ingredients, except the garnishes, stirring well. Serve in Mason jars on the rocks. Garnish with candy on skewers or floating in each cocktail.

Yields 6 to 8 cocktails.

Harvest Moon

The melded flavors of pumpkin and cinnamon-infused moonshine with a spot of honey are the best way to welcome cool autumn nights while lounging under a harvest moon.

- 2 ounces pumpkin puree
- 3 ounces cinnamon-infused moonshine (p. 160)
- ½ to 1 teaspoon pumpkin pie spice
- ½ to 1 teaspoon honey

In a shaker filled with ice, combine all the ingredients, shaking well. Strain into a Mason jar.

Yields 1 cocktail.

Dandelion and Honey Iced Tea

Whether you're currently rooted along a dirt road or amidst the hustle and bustle of city streets, this spiked dandelion and honey iced tea tastes like home sweet home.

- 8 cups boiling water
- 6 dandelion root teabags
- 2 cups dandelion-infused moonshine (p. 166) or honey-infused moonshine (p. 168), or to taste
- 8 teaspoons honey, or to taste

In a large pitcher, add the boiling water and teabags. Let steep for 30 minutes. In a refrigerator, chill the dandelion tea (leave in the teabags) for 1 or more hours.

To serve, remove the teabags from the pitcher. Fill chilled Mason jars halfway with ice. Pour ¼ cup, or more to taste, of the moonshine into each jar. Add a teaspoon of honey to each jar. Fill the remainder of each jar with the dandelion tea. Stir to combine. Add more honey, if desired.

Yields 8 cocktails.

White Chocolate Moontini

With the help of white chocolate liqueur and rebel's choice of chocolate or strawberry syrup, decadence meets moonshine in this eyes-rolled-back-in-your-head twist on one of the most popular martinis on the planet.

- 1 ½ ounces cocoa-infused moonshine (p. 162) or mint-infused moonshine (p. 158)
- 3 ounces white chocolate liqueur
- Chocolate or strawberry syrup

In a shaker filled with ice, add the moonshine and liqueur, shaking until well blended. Strain the mixture into a small, chilled Mason jar, over ice if desired. Drizzle the top with the chocolate or strawberry syrup.

Yields 1 cocktail.

Alabama Shiner

The amaretto, sloe gin, grenadine, and OJ of the famous Alabama Slammer just got a bootlegger's 180 twist with doses of peach liqueur and almond-infused moonshine.

- ½ ounce almond-infused moonshine (p. 127)
- ½ ounce amaretto
- ½ ounce peach liqueur
- ½ ounce sloe gin
- ½ ounce grenadine
- 2 ounces orange juice
- ¼ ounce sweet and sour mix

In a shaker filled with ice, combine all the ingredients, shaking well. Strain into a Mason jar.

Yields 1 cocktail.

Acknowledgments

With a raised Mason jar of XXX, I would like to toast and thank the team of fellow rebel spirits who helped me to put this book into your hands . . .

My literary agents, Steve Troha and Erin Niumata at Folio Literary Management, who championed this project from the very beginning.

My editor, Denise Silvestro at Kensington/Citadel, whose sharp eye and kind heart helped shape this unique combination of history and cocktails into an informative, inspiring, and entertaining book that will be enjoyed (*and imbibed!*) for generations to come.

The PR, Marketing, and Sales teams at Kensington/Citadel— namely Vida Engstrand, Jane Nutter, Michelle Addo, and Darla Freeman, who are among the best of the best in their tireless efforts to help me share this book with the world and ensure the celebration never ends.

The several others at Kensington/Citadel— namely Steven Zacharius, Lynn Cully, Adam Zacharius, Barbara Bennett, and Jackie Dinas who understand the power of the written word to educate, inspire, and entertain, and who saw those very percolations within these pages from Day One.

The design team at Koechel Peterson and Associates—namely John Peterson, Dave Koechel, and Gregory Rohm, who brilliantly took my words and my recipes, along with incredible photography, and translated them into a *buzz-worthy* work of art that will brighten the hearts and rebel spirits of readers everywhere.

Amy Beadle Roth, who styled and shot the most incredible cocktail photographs, elevating the art form to a whole new level as only she can.

The following organizations, who each supplied historical photos, helping to make this book the first time this specifically curated collection of moonshine photos has ever been published in one place: Georgia Archives; Kansas State Historical Society; Kentucky Historical Society; Minnesota Historical Society; NASCAR Hall of Fame; State Archives of North Carolina; Tennessee State Library and Archives; The Filson Historical Society; and West Virginia State Archives.

And, finally, a BIG ROUND OF APPLAUSE to the moonshiners, who, for more than 200 years, have taught us all how to embrace an independent and entrepreneurial spirit of fun, mischief, and living life to the fullest!

About the Author

John Schlimm is a Harvard-trained educator, artist, award-winning writer, and a member of one of the oldest and most historic brewing families in the U.S. (Straub Brewery, founded by his great-great-grandfather in the 1870s).

The consummate storyteller, John is a critically-acclaimed essayist and author of 17 previous books, including his Christopher Award-winning memoir *Five Years in Heaven* and several boozy cookbooks such as *The Ultimate Beer Lover's Happy Hour*, *The Tipsy Vegan*, and *The Ultimate Beer Lover's Cookbook*, which is the largest beer cookbook ever published and was awarded "Best Beer Book in the World" and "Best Beer Book in the U.S." by Gourmand International.

John has appeared on such national media outlets as *The Ellen DeGeneres Show*, Bravo's *Watch What Happens Live*, NPR, Martha Stewart Living's *Everyday Food*, *The Splendid Table*, QVC, and *Fox & Friends*.

For more information and to connect with John on social media, please visit www.JohnSchlimm.com.

"With *Moonshine*, my goal was to create the ultimate 180-proof party in a book!"

Photo Credits

Pages 12-13: Courtesy, Georgia Archives, Vanishing Georgia Collection, mur109-82wm_72

Page 16: Courtesy, Georgia Archives, Vanishing Georgia Collection, gil001wm_72

Page 20: The Filson Historical Society, Louisville, KY, DIS-22

Page 23: Courtesy, Georgia Archives, Vanishing Georgia Collection, emn053wm_72

Page 26: "Looking Back at Tennessee" Photograph Collection c1890-1981, Courtesy of Tennessee State Library and Archives, 11866

Page 28: Courtesy of Kansas State Historical Society, 00379065

Page 33: Mike Gioulis Collection, West Virginia State Archives, 042913

Pages 34-35: West Virginia State Police Collection, West Virginia State Archives, 237013

Page 36: "Looking Back at Tennessee" Photograph Collection c1890-1981, Courtesy of Tennessee State Library and Archives, 8960

Page 39: Courtesy of the State Archives of North Carolina, N_71_11_153

Page 44: Courtesy of the Minnesota Historical Society

Page 47: Fleta Sager Shobe Collection, West Virginia State Archives, 067901

Page 48: Courtesy of the State Archives of North Carolina, N_2005_1_2

Page 52: Courtesy of Kansas State Historical Society, 00474233

Page 54: West Virginia State Police Collection, West Virginia State Archives, 237001

Page 61: Courtesy of Kentucky Historical Society, Graphic22_Box1_6_4

Page 63: Robert R. Keller Collection, West Virginia State Archives, 081801

Page 66: "Looking Back at Tennessee" Photograph Collection c1890-1981, Courtesy of Tennessee State Library and Archives, 6313

Page 75: Courtesy, Georgia Archives, Vanishing Georgia Collection, was306wm_72

Page 76: Courtesy of Kentucky Historical Society, Graphic22_Box1_6_5

Page 85: Courtesy of the State Archives of North Carolina, N_89_3_12

Page 86: "Looking Back at Tennessee" Photograph Collection c1890-1981, Courtesy of Tennessee State Library and Archives, 6327

Page 90: Fern See Collection, West Virginia State Archives, 088811

Page 94: Olin Ruth Collection, West Virginia State Archives, 128109

Page 100: Photo courtesy of nascarhall.com, NASCAR Hall of Fame

Page 103: Olin Ruth Collection, West Virginia State Archives, 128110

Cocktail photos by Amy Beadle Roth: *Pages 106, 110, 136, 152, 172, 182, 188, 194, 200, 206, 212, 218, 224, 230, 236*

Author photo by John Schlimm: *Page 252*

Cheers!